INTERNATIONAL DEVELOPMENT IN PRACTICE

A Guiding Framework for Nutrition Public Expenditure Reviews

HUIHUI WANG, KYOKO SHIBATA OKAMURA,
ALI WINOTO SUBANDORO, YURIE TANIMICHI HOBERG,
LUBINA FATIMAH QURESHY, AND MAMATA GHIMIRE

© 2022 International Bank for Reconstruction and Development / The World Bank
1818 H Street NW, Washington, DC 20433
Telephone: 202-473-1000; Internet: www.worldbank.org

Some rights reserved

1 2 3 4   25 24 23 22

Books in this series are published to communicate the results of Bank research, analysis, and operational experience with the least possible delay. The extent of language editing varies from book to book.

This work is a product of the staff of The World Bank with external contributions. The findings, interpretations, and conclusions expressed in this work do not necessarily reflect the views of The World Bank, its Board of Executive Directors, or the governments they represent. The World Bank does not guarantee the accuracy, completeness, or currency of the data included in this work and does not assume responsibility for any errors, omissions, or discrepancies in the information, or liability with respect to the use of or failure to use the information, methods, processes, or conclusions set forth. The boundaries, colors, denominations, and other information shown on any map in this work do not imply any judgment on the part of The World Bank concerning the legal status of any territory or the endorsement or acceptance of such boundaries.

Nothing herein shall constitute or be construed or considered to be a limitation upon or waiver of the privileges and immunities of The World Bank, all of which are specifically reserved.

Rights and Permissions

This work is available under the Creative Commons Attribution 3.0 IGO license (CC BY 3.0 IGO) http://creativecommons.org/licenses/by/3.0/igo. Under the Creative Commons Attribution license, you are free to copy, distribute, transmit, and adapt this work, including for commercial purposes, under the following conditions:

Attribution—Please cite the work as follows: Wang, Huihui, Kyoko Shibata Okamura, Ali Winoto Subandoro, Yurie Tanimichi Hoberg, Lubina Fatimah Qureshy, and Mamata Ghimire. 2022. *A Guiding Framework for Nutrition Public Expenditure Reviews*. International Development in Practice. Washington, DC: World Bank. doi:10.1596/978-1-4648-1853-0. License: Creative Commons Attribution CC BY 3.0 IGO

Translations—If you create a translation of this work, please add the following disclaimer along with the attribution: *This translation was not created by The World Bank and should not be considered an official World Bank translation. The World Bank shall not be liable for any content or error in this translation.*

Adaptations—If you create an adaptation of this work, please add the following disclaimer along with the attribution: *This is an adaptation of an original work by The World Bank. Views and opinions expressed in the adaptation are the sole responsibility of the author or authors of the adaptation and are not endorsed by The World Bank.*

Third-party content—The World Bank does not necessarily own each component of the content contained within the work. The World Bank therefore does not warrant that the use of any third-party-owned individual component or part contained in the work will not infringe on the rights of those third parties. The risk of claims resulting from such infringement rests solely with you. If you wish to re-use a component of the work, it is your responsibility to determine whether permission is needed for that re-use and to obtain permission from the copyright owner. Examples of components can include, but are not limited to, tables, figures, or images.

All queries on rights and licenses should be addressed to World Bank Publications, The World Bank Group, 1818 H Street NW, Washington, DC 20433, USA; e-mail: pubrights@worldbank.org.

ISBN: 978-1-4648-1853-0
DOI: 10.1596/978-1-4648-1853-0

Cover photo: © Lucian Coman / Shutterstock. Used with permission; further permission required for reuse.
Cover design: Debra Naylor / Naylor Design Inc.

Contents

Acknowledgments   vii
About the Authors   ix
Overview: About This Book   xi
Abbreviations   xv

CHAPTER 1 **Introduction**   1
Global context for nutrition financing   1
Landscape of nutrition budget and expenditure analysis work   2
Why an NPER?   4
Notes   6
References   6

CHAPTER 2 **Preparation Phase**   7
Defining the scope   7
Establishing an NPER team   9
Preparing a work plan   10
Identifying data sources   11
Notes   14
References   15

CHAPTER 3 **Key Elements of an NPER**   17
Country context   17
National nutrition strategy   19
Institutional framework and budget process   20
Identifying nutrition expenditures   23
Analysis   32
Composition of expenditures   33
Notes   48
References   50

CHAPTER 4 **Using the NPER for Greater Impact**   53
The way forward on policy dialogue and institutional strengthening   53
Improving the quality of future NPERs   54
Note   55

APPENDIX A **Framework for Actions to Achieve Optimum Fetal and Child Nutrition and Development, as Published in *The Lancet*: *The Lancet Framework*   57**

APPENDIX B Results Structure of the Nepal Multi-Sector Nutrition Plan: 2018–2022   59

APPENDIX C List of NPERs and Other Related Documents   63

Boxes

1.1 NPERs and their role in promoting policy dialogue   5
2.1 Lead government entities involved in existing nutrition public expenditure reviews   9
2.2 Experience from the Bangladesh NPER on estimating donor funding for nutrition investments implemented by nongovernmental organizations   13
3.1 How NPERs are aligned with national nutrition policy goals   20
3.2 Examples of keywords used in the Bhutan NPER, by sector/ministry   27
3.3 Example from Indonesia of how to perform a keyword search on multiple data sets   27
3.4 Guidance on high-cost, nutrition-sensitive budget line items   29
3.5 Using weights to assess the contribution of Indonesia's National Health Insurance   30
3.6 Assessing the effectiveness of health spending in Mozambique   39
3.7 Potential bottlenecks in the flow of funds in Indonesia   44
3.8 Collecting data on off-budget external nutrition financing in Rwanda   45

Figures

O.1 Conceptual structure of NPERs   xii
2.1 Nutrition activities span different government levels and multiple line ministries   8
3.1 Example from the Indonesia NPER: Stunting rate relative to comparators   18
3.2 Example from the Bhutan NPER: Stunting by region, area, age, and wealth   19
3.3 Example from the Tanzania NPER: Budget process diagram   22
3.4 Example from the Indonesia NPER: Flow of nutrition financing   23
3.5 Flow chart of steps to identify nutrition expenditures   24
3.6 Breakdown of nutrition-specific and nutrition-sensitive spending   35
B3.6.1 Health spending per capita in Mozambique, by key outcome, 1995–2013   39
3.7 Example from the Rwanda NPER: Optima simulation result   41
3.8 Example from the Bhutan NPER: Absorption rates for nutrition-related interventions by ministry   43
3.9 Example from the Indonesia NPER: Budget execution by intervention   43
3.10 Example from the Ethiopia health sector PER: External assistance managed by the Ministry of Health   45
3.11 Example from the Tanzania NPER: District-level nutrition spending per child under five plotted against the stunting rate   46

Tables

3.1 Example from the Indonesia NPER: Nutrition-related interventions   25
3.2 The *Lancet* framework for programs and interventions, by nutrition category   26
B3.4.1 NPER examples of the use of weights as proxies for nutrition contributions   29
3.3 Use of disaggregation weights for bundled budgets   31
3.4 Selected key metrics in NPERs   32
3.5 Breakdown of expenditures by broad nutrition categories   34
3.6 Results framework of Nepal's Multi-Sector Nutrition Plan: 2018–2022   37
3.7 Example from the Bhutan NPER: Subnational nutrition-related expenditures, 2016–17   46

3.8	Example from the Zambia health sector PER: BIA results on the distribution of outpatient and inpatient services 47
C.1	Nutrition public expenditure reviews 63
C.2	Related documents: nutrition financing tracking, sector public expenditure reviews with nutrition coverage 63

Acknowledgments

This guiding framework for nutrition public expenditure reviews was prepared by a World Bank and Global Financing Facility (GFF) team of Mamata Ghimire (consultant, World Bank), Yurie Tanimichi Hoberg (consultant, World Bank), Kyoko Shibata Okamura (nutrition specialist, World Bank), Lubina Fatimah Qureshy (consultant, World Bank), and Ali Winoto Subandoro (senior nutrition specialist, GFF), led by Huihui Wang (senior economist/task team leader, World Bank). Overall guidance was provided by Meera Shekar (global lead for nutrition, World Bank). Kseniya Bieliaieva and Juliana Williams of the World Bank provided administrative support. The report has benefited from thoughtful peer review comments from Annalies Borrel (UNICEF), Zelalem Yilma Debebe (World Bank), Augustin Flory (Results for Development), and Patrick Hoang-Vu Eozenou (World Bank), as well as substantive technical comments from Xiaohui Hou, Yi-Kyoung Lee, Moritz Piatti, Denise Silfverberg, and Ajay Tandon, all from the World Bank.

Financial support for this work was provided by the Government of Japan through the Japan Trust Fund for Scaling Up Nutrition.

About the Authors

Mamata Ghimire is a health economist with expertise in the areas of health financing, nutrition financing, public expenditure reviews, and surveys. She has worked in the South Asia, West Africa, and East Asia and Pacific regions. Her experience spans high-quality analytical work and internationally visible research, advisory services, and lending operations. She holds a PhD in health economics.

Lubina Fatimah Qureshy has moved from an initial interest in the economics of health to an increased focus on nutrition economics. Her recent work encompasses modeling the economic impact of food fortification, modeling stunting projections, cost-benefit analyses of nutrition investment projects, nutrition budgetary analysis, and nutrition financing. She has worked on projects in India, Indonesia, Mozambique, Papua New Guinea, and Timor-Leste. She holds a master's degree and PhD in economics from the University of Sussex.

Kyoko Shibata Okamura has worked in the areas of health policy research, large-scale nutrition program management in Asia and Africa, nutrition financing and accountability, and nutrition-sensitive agriculture and food systems. She joined the Global Engagement Unit of the World Bank's Health, Nutrition, and Population Global Practice in 2018, working on nutrition financing and service delivery, obesity prevention strategies, and the nutrition and food systems nexus, among other issues, in addition to providing technical support for nutrition operations in countries. She holds a master's degree in health science from the Johns Hopkins Bloomberg School of Public Health.

Ali Winoto Subandoro is a senior nutrition specialist in the Global Financing Facility (GFF) of the World Bank. Ali has over 20 years of experience working in low- and middle-income countries focusing on nutrition service delivery, financing, and governance. Ali joined the GFF Secretariat in the World Bank's Health, Nutrition, and Population Global Practice in 2017. He manages GFF portfolios in Ghana, Indonesia, and Rwanda, supporting countries to accelerate progress in reproductive, maternal, neonatal, child, and adolescent health and nutrition. He leads operational and technical work on nutrition financing and governance, integration of nutrition in health systems, and multisectoral approaches to nutrition. Ali holds a master's degree in economics from the London School of Economics and Political Science.

Yurie Tanimichi Hoberg is a consultant at the World Bank. Previously, she was a senior economist in the Global Engagement unit in the Agriculture and Food Global Practice of the World Bank. Her expert areas include global food security policy, nutrition-sensitive agriculture, and results monitoring for agriculture projects. She has significant operational experience in World Bank global partnerships, such as the Global Agriculture and Food Security Program, FoodSystems 2030, the Forest Carbon Partnership Facility, and the Green Climate Fund. She holds a PhD in agricultural and resource economics from the University of California, Berkeley.

Huihui Wang is a senior economist in the Health, Nutrition, and Population Global Practice of the World Bank. She has 20 years of experience working in low-, middle-, and high-income countries with a focus on supporting them to achieve universal health coverage. She led the World Bank's lending operations and technical support in health system strengthening and reforms in the East Asia, Europe and Central Asia, and Africa regions. She is leading global initiatives related to transforming and improving primary health care, knowledge programs on COVID-19 (coronavirus) response and health system resilience, and financing for nutrition. She has a multidisciplinary background: a medical degree from Beijing Medical University, a master's degree in economics, and a PhD in health services and policy analysis from the University of California, Berkeley.

Overview: About This Book

The main purpose of this book is to present the key elements of a nutrition public expenditure review (NPER) and offer a guiding framework, practical steps, and examples for carrying out an NPER. It targets a wide-ranging audience, including country nutrition policy makers, development partners, government technical staff, and advocates and practitioners tasked with carrying out NPERs (who are also the main target audience). The guiding framework draws upon good practices from the growing body of NPERs as well as common practices and expertise from public expenditure reviews (PERs). However, given the limited number of existing NPERs, this book should be considered a starting point, or a "living document," and is not meant to provide comprehensive coverage of a standard methodology for NPERs, since that would require further work and analysis.

Specifically, this guiding framework aims to be a useful tool for practitioners involved in developing an NPER. It does this by (1) situating NPERs within the context of other similar efforts, such as a nutrition budget analysis or sector-specific PERs; (2) presenting the literature on existing NPERs and related literature to serve as a reference; (3) providing guidance on preparatory work before beginning an NPER (that is, defining the scope, setting up an NPER team, and identifying data sources); (4) providing guidance on conducting the core analysis (that is, framing the analysis, analyzing the institutional framework, and linking the analysis to the policy dialogue); and (5) clearly identifying knowledge gaps and necessary additional work to enhance the robustness of future NPER analyses.

NPERs determine the level of a country's overall nutrition public spending and assess whether the expenditure profile is fit-for-purpose for the country to achieve its nutritional goals and objectives. However, this type of assessment requires access to sufficient quality data and adequate technical capacity on the NPER team as well as among supporting stakeholders, especially with data collection and cleaning.

When data availability or data quality is an issue or technical capacity is lacking, NPER teams may need to limit the scope of the study. Figure O.1 presents the broad conceptual structure and some related questions that underpin NPERs. A full-fledged NPER aims to explain how financing ultimately leads to desired outputs by presenting information on three main sequential

FIGURE O.1
Conceptual structure of NPERs

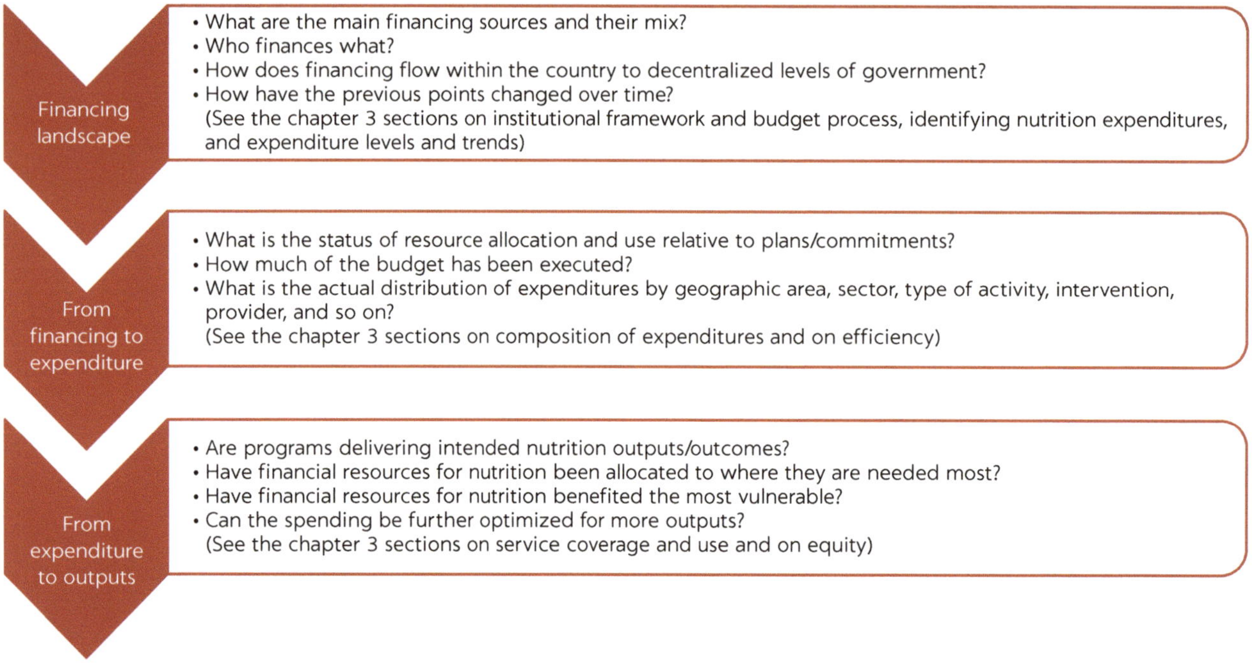

Financing landscape
- What are the main financing sources and their mix?
- Who finances what?
- How does financing flow within the country to decentralized levels of government?
- How have the previous points changed over time?
(See the chapter 3 sections on institutional framework and budget process, identifying nutrition expenditures, and expenditure levels and trends)

From financing to expenditure
- What is the status of resource allocation and use relative to plans/commitments?
- How much of the budget has been executed?
- What is the actual distribution of expenditures by geographic area, sector, type of activity, intervention, provider, and so on?
(See the chapter 3 sections on composition of expenditures and on efficiency)

From expenditure to outputs
- Are programs delivering intended nutrition outputs/outcomes?
- Have financial resources for nutrition been allocated to where they are needed most?
- Have financial resources for nutrition benefited the most vulnerable?
- Can the spending be further optimized for more outputs?
(See the chapter 3 sections on service coverage and use and on equity)

Source: World Bank.

Note: Listed questions are indicative (not comprehensive). A more comprehensive list of questions is included at the beginning of each section in chapter 3, starting from the section on the institutional framework and budget process. NPER = nutrition public expenditure review.

building blocks: financing landscape, from financing to expenditures, and from expenditures to outputs. In a less ideal situation, teams may choose to limit the scope of the study to only one or two of these building blocks and postpone a full NPER until data or capacity constraints have been addressed.

To inform future NPER teams and aid them in deciding a feasible scope, this book presents data and analytical challenges that were faced by previous NPER teams. It shows the kinds of analyses that NPERs have been able to carry out and those that they were unable to perform because of data or capacity constraints. It is important to note that, because of a lack of a high-quality data, no NPER to date has carried out some key analyses, such as an effectiveness analysis or technical efficiency analysis (which are commonly undertaken in PERs).

In its final chapter, this book presents further work at both the global and country levels that is needed to create the conditions necessary to carry out more comprehensive NPERs. As of December 2021, only seven NPERs have been completed, and none of them has successfully examined all the standard PER analysis of effectiveness, efficiency, and equity. Therefore, more work by technical and financial stakeholders in the global nutrition community is urgently needed to enable more comprehensive NPERs to be undertaken in the future. As such, this book is expected to be updated periodically in the form of a living document with revised and updated guidance, and relevant new information and experience from future NPERs.

Finally, this book is structured in the following way. Chapter 1 (introduction) presents the complementarity and value added offered by NPERs to existing analytical tools, such as the Scaling Up Nutrition budget analysis, Systems of

Health Accounts framework, and other nutrition-sensitive sectoral PERs. Chapter 2 (preparation phase) lays out issues that the NPER should address before conducting the study, such as defining the scope, developing an inclusive NPER team, and drafting a work plan. Chapter 3 (key elements of an NPER) presents the various parts of a comprehensive NPER, from a description of the country context to the standard analysis of effectiveness, efficiency, and equity. Finally, the document concludes with chapter 4 (using the NPER for greater impact), which identifies future work that is needed to overcome current constraints and enable more robust analyses in future NPERs.

Abbreviations

BIA	benefit incidence analysis
DEA	data envelopment analysis
DHS	Demographic and Health Surveys
DP	development partner
FMIS	financial management information system
HC PEIR	human capital public expenditure and institutional review
IFMIS	integrated financial management information system
IYCF	infant and young child feeding
JKN	Jaminan Kesehatan Nasional (National Health Insurance, Indonesia)
MICS	Multiple Indicator Cluster Surveys
NGO	nongovernmental organization
NHA	National Health Accounts
NPER	nutrition public expenditure review
Nu	Bhutanese ngultrum
PER	public expenditure review
PFM	public financial management
Rp	Indonesian rupiah
SHA	System of Health Accounts
SPRING	Strengthening Partnerships, Results, and Innovations in Nutrition Globally
SUN	Scaling Up Nutrition
T Sh	Tanzania shilling

Introduction

GLOBAL CONTEXT FOR NUTRITION FINANCING

Nutrition investments affect human capital formation, which in turn affects economic growth. Malnutrition is intrinsically connected to human capital because undernutrition contributes to 45 percent of child mortality and because stunting is known to be associated with lost productivity and earnings in adulthood (Shekar et al. 2017). Moreover, one in five adult deaths can be attributed to dietary risk factors. Nutrition investments, particularly in the first 1,000 days of a person's life, yield high returns and have proven to be cost-effective.[1] Two landmark reports from the World Bank, *Scaling Up Nutrition: What Will It Cost?* (Horton et al. 2010) and *An Investment Framework for Nutrition* (Shekar et al. 2017), shed light on the costs of scaling up high-impact nutrition interventions to achieve the global nutrition targets endorsed by the World Health Assembly in 2012, and which have since been adopted as the Sustainable Development Goals' nutrition targets for 2030.

Growing recognition of the value of investments in nutrition, its multisectoral nature, and the need for stronger coordination and accountability mechanisms led to the establishment of the current global architecture for nutrition. Appendix A presents a framework for actions to achieve optimum fetal and child nutrition and development, as published in *The Lancet* (Black et al. 2013), which illustrates the multisectoral dimension of nutrition as represented by both nutrition-specific and nutrition-sensitive interventions. The Scaling Up Nutrition (SUN) movement was launched in 2010 as a unique global movement to catalyze support for countries prepared to "scale up nutrition" through a multisectoral and multistakeholder approach that involves networks of governments, development partners, foundations, civil society organizations, and business entities.[2] In 2013, the Nutrition for Growth initiative was launched, whereby governments, development partners, and business and civil society leaders convene a summit every four years and publicly announce commitments to nutrition policies.[3] The commitments, including financial commitments, made by the participating stakeholders are followed up through several forums and analytical work, including the annual *Global Nutrition Report*, which gathers and publishes information on progress made against those commitments.[4] One of the main goals of the *Global Nutrition Report* is to promote global accountability for nutrition investments and results.

Despite these efforts, high-quality data on nutrition-related financing are scarce, making it difficult to assess the level and effectiveness of investments. The World Bank's Investment Framework for Nutrition estimated the need for an additional US$7 billion per year in high-impact, nutrition-specific interventions to achieve the global targets for stunting, anemia in women, exclusive breastfeeding, and the scaling up of the treatment of severe wasting (Shekar et al. 2017). Recognizing the underfunding of nutrition interventions and a lack of reliable financing information and accountability, the Nutrition for Growth Summit in Tokyo in 2021 focused on the need for effective and sustainable financing for nutrition (that is, "more money for nutrition and more nutrition for the money spent"). However, tracking the expenditures of multisectoral interventions, such as nutrition-related investments, requires significantly more work than sector-specific expenditures, such as investments in agriculture, education, or health. Even though it is an important step in operationalizing their commitments to achieving the World Health Assembly's and Sustainable Development Goals' nutrition targets through a multisectoral approach, most countries do not quantify the level and distribution of public financing for nutrition. Put simply, there are many more unknowns in the basic parameters of nutrition financing (for example, what is being spent and by whom and on what?) compared to traditional sectors, each of which is often governed by a single ministry.

LANDSCAPE OF NUTRITION BUDGET AND EXPENDITURE ANALYSIS WORK

The 2020 *Global Nutrition Report* states that sparse data on nutrition-related financing—which (when available) are often disparate, incomplete, or incomparable—make it almost impossible to accurately track progress in nutrition investments (Development Initiatives 2020). However, in recent years, efforts have increased significantly to improve the availability of information on nutrition financing from domestic and development partner sources. They include the SUN budget analysis; the nutrition budgeting and financial analysis of the Strengthening Partnerships, Results, and Innovations in Nutrition Globally (SPRING) project funded by the United States Agency for International Development; analyses of the World Health Organization–supported System of Health Accounts (SHA) data; and nutrition-focused public expenditure reviews (PERs) conducted by the World Bank and the United Nations Children's Fund either as stand-alone nutrition public expenditure reviews (NPERs), as part of a broader exercise such as the human capital public expenditure and institutional reviews (HC PEIRs), or as sector-specific PERs that include some examination of nutrition spending.

SUN budget analysis. The SUN budget analysis exercise, which has been conducted in 50 countries to date, is based on self-reporting by governments and uses an Excel template and guidelines provided by the SUN Secretariat (Fracassi et al. 2020; MQSUN+ 2020). It focuses on assessing budget allocations instead of on actual spending. The relatively light requirement of the

SUN budget analysis has allowed it to be rolled out in many countries in a relatively short time, making valuable contributions in terms of mobilizing attention to country-level nutrition financing and accountability needs. However, it does not cover the full public financial management (PFM) process, including accounting for actual spending, nor does it include a full and robust analysis of the effectiveness, efficiency, and equity of public expenditures. Nevertheless, the three-step methodology of identifying, categorizing, and analyzing nutrition budgets developed for the SUN budget analysis has gone through multiple revisions since it was introduced in 2015; and it was used as the basis for the SPRING work in Nepal and Uganda (the SPRING project closed in 2018), as well as for most NPERs (to quantify nutrition-related expenditures), with some country-specific customization.

SHA. The World Health Organization–supported SHA tracks health funding and expenditures and disaggregates data on nutrition. The SHA provides an internationally standardized framework for the systematic measurement of health care revenues and expenditures, including nutrition, and the comparison of results over time and across countries. However, the SHA monitors nutrition expenditures only within the health sector and does not cover important nutrition investments in other sectors. Moreover, the SHA assigns only one code for all expenditures related to nutritional diseases, which does not allow for an analysis of specific categories such as nutrition-specific or nutrition-sensitive interventions, major intervention packages defined in the national health or nutrition plan, and so on.

The World Bank's HC PEIR. The HC PEIR applies a cross-cutting human capital lens to assess the contributions of public expenditures and institutions to a set of country-specific human capital outcomes, including nutrition. It examines expenditure levels, trends, distribution, sufficiency/sustainability, and efficiency/equity as well as expenditure alignment, complementarity, and optimization across sectors toward human capital outcomes. It also identifies institutional bottlenecks to translating policies, programs, and expenditures into outcomes. Moreover, the HC PEIR analyzes the enabling environment for the acceleration of human capital outcomes with regard to political economy, social norms and values, and demand-side factors. The World Bank is rolling out HC PEIRs in selected countries: Argentina (province of Mendoza), Bangladesh, Burkina Faso, Kenya, and Togo.

Sector-specific PERs that include some analysis of nutrition. A PER is a standard World Bank analytical work that serves as a diagnostic tool for countries to investigate the use of public finances in meeting policy priorities. A general PER assesses governmentwide expenditures. Sectoral PERs focus on specific themes or sectors such as health, education, agriculture, or water. Examples to date of sector-specific PERs that have some analysis of nutrition include agriculture sector PERs (Lesotho and Rwanda), early childhood development PERs (Paraguay), and health sector PERs (Zambia). These sector PERs provide insights into nutrition-related expenditures within the respective sector, but they do not provide a full picture of the total nutrition expenditure program (and its impact) that spans multiple sectors. The nutrition analysis embedded in these sector PERs also tends to be disjointed from the main PER analysis and treated as a less detailed add-on exercise to the main sectoral analysis.

WHY AN NPER?

When done well, an NPER goes beyond simply quantifying how much is allocated or spent on nutrition; it answers how well money is being spent to achieve nutrition outcomes and identifies specific recommendations for improvement. The NPER process involves identifying and analyzing nutrition-related expenditures through commonly accepted methodologies (for example, the SUN methodology) that are adapted to the country context.

An NPER is different from sector-specific PERs in that nutrition expenditures span many sectors. An NPER offers a quantitative evaluation of a country's nutrition-related public expenditures through a multisectoral analysis of its financial data and investigates if the expenditures served to improve nutrition outcomes. Its ultimate utility lies in the ability to interpret the results of the analysis to guide policy making (Pradhan 1996). However, NPERs explore the association between financing and intended outcomes, not causality. This means that NPERs do not strive to determine the attribution of a specific intervention or program toward outcomes, which is the domain of impact evaluation studies.

Some expected benefits of NPERs:

- They provide an opportunity to extend the policy dialogue on nutrition by engaging ministries of finance or planning and key line ministries in multisectoral discussions on nutrition change policies and their fiscal implications.
- They produce a clear analysis of the effectiveness, efficiency, and equity of public expenditures on nutrition to formulate evidence-based, actionable recommendations on strategic resource allocation or course corrections.
- They provide an opportunity to develop or strengthen a country's nutrition strategy and associated costed investment plans by illustrating how actual expenditures are supporting these strategies.
- They promote transparency (through publication and consultation) in what constitutes nutrition spending and prevent overestimating by applying evidence-based weights to budget line items that are not sufficiently disaggregated in budget data.
- They help mobilize domestic and external resources for the nutrition agenda by highlighting policy objectives that require additional financing. For external financing, the NPER informs the government's dialogue with development partners on identifying development assistance priorities and areas in need of external financing.
- They highlight the strengths and weaknesses of the institutional framework for addressing nutrition.
- They become an entry point for future work on strengthening the overall PFM cycle—budget tagging, tracking, and evaluation—to mainstream the tracking of nutrition expenditures.

Ultimately, NPERs aim to carry out an in-depth analysis of the effectiveness, efficiency, and equity of nutrition-related public spending to formulate evidence-based, actionable recommendations on strategic resource allocation or course corrections (box 1.1). The existing portfolio of NPERs is small (there have been only seven NPERs to date), and none of them has included an in-depth analysis of the effectiveness, efficiency, or equity of nutrition expenditures, mainly because of a lack of access to disaggregated data.

> **BOX 1.1**
>
> ### NPERs and their role in promoting policy dialogue
>
> Nutrition public expenditure reviews (NPERs) are fairly new public expenditure tools (the oldest NPER was published in 2018). To date, NPERs have been completed in Bangladesh (Finance Division, Government of the Republic of Bangladesh and UNICEF 2019), Bhutan (Ahmed et al. 2020), Indonesia (World Bank 2020a), Nepal (World Bank 2019), Rwanda (Piatti-Fünfkirchen et al. 2020), Sri Lanka (World Bank 2020b), and Tanzania (Tanzania MoFP and UNICEF 2018) (see appendix C for a complete list).
>
> NPERs are being used as entry points for broadening the policy dialogue on nutrition in their respective countries to strengthen public financial management and achieve better nutrition results:
>
> - In Bangladesh, the NPER facilitated a major policy shift to focus on aligning program design for improving nutrition in key sectors. For instance, the Bangladesh National Nutrition Council and the Cabinet Division (under the Prime Minister's office responsible for overall coordination among all ministries) have carried out a review of major social safety net programs to make them nutrition and gender sensitive, and they have agreed to include a nutrition chapter in the upcoming revision of the National Social Security Strategy.
> - In Indonesia, the findings from the NPER informed the policy dialogue on addressing several systemic challenges in public financial management, such as delays in fund transfers and a weak focus on results in the planning and budgeting process, which results in spending inefficiency. The NPER also highlighted challenges with tracking subnational spending due to the lack of a standardized chart of account across districts.
> - In Rwanda, the NPER contributed to advancing the dialogue with the Ministry of Finance to strengthen nutrition-responsive budgeting and adopt policy reforms related to budget tagging, tracking, and evaluation, which in turn will enable the government to oversee nutrition-related activities across all agency budgets and levels of government.

NPERs also shed light on institutional aspects that may affect nutrition outcomes. This role is particularly important for a multisectoral agenda such as nutrition, which is often seen as "somebody else's agenda." NPERs describe the flow of funds to public nutrition-related interventions and identify bottlenecks that may be preventing the country's PFM systems from optimizing planning, budgeting, and spending for nutrition. For example, in Rwanda, the findings from the NPER informed the scope of additional work on strengthening the nutrition-responsive PFM system. This work included the issuance of a Ministerial Instruction by the Ministry of Finance during the planning and budgeting phase to (1) instruct relevant ministries and agencies to consider early childhood development throughout the budget process, and (2) ensure that activities are prioritized and aligned with the National Early Childhood Development Program, which coordinates all nutrition activities in the country.

The COVID-19 (coronavirus) pandemic has served as a reminder that the ability to track and measure the impact of public spending on nutrition is important during economic or social crises. During such crises, governments often struggle to balance the implementation of urgent, short-term emergency response measures with maintaining medium- to long-term policies aimed at protecting the vulnerable from the impact of malnutrition and human capital loss. NPERs can help governments identify, track, evaluate, and plan public spending on key nutrition measures and assist efforts to hold both financiers and implementers accountable.

NOTES

1. *The Lancet* Maternal and Child Nutrition series of 2008 and 2013.
2. For more information, see the SUN website (https://scalingupnutrition.org/).
3. For more information, see the Nutrition for Growth website (https://nutritionforgrowth.org/).
4. For more on the *Global Nutrition Report* and the commitment tracker, see the *Global Nutrition Report* website (https://globalnutritionreport.org/resources/nutrition-growth-commitment-tracking/).

REFERENCES

Ahmed, S., M. Bhattarai, D. Drakpa, L. Dzed, M. Ghimire, P. Lhazon, A. Tandon, and V. Ulep. 2020. "'What Gets Measured Gets Managed': Assessing Public Financing for Improving Nutrition Outcomes and Human Capital in Bhutan." Health, Nutrition, and Population Discussion Paper, World Bank, Washington, DC.

Black, R., C. Victora, S. Walker, Z. Bhutta, P. Christian, M. De Onis, R. Uauy, et al. 2013. "Maternal and Child Undernutrition and Overweight in Low-Income and Middle-Income Countries." *The Lancet* 382 (9890): 427–51.

Development Initiatives. 2020. *Global Nutrition Report: Action on Equity to End Malnutrition*. Bristol: Development Initiatives. https://globalnutritionreport.org/reports/2020-global-nutrition-report/.

Finance Division, Government of the Republic of Bangladesh and UNICEF (United Nations Children's Fund). 2019. *Bangladesh Public Expenditure Review on Nutrition*. Dhaka: Government of Bangladesh and UNICEF.

Fracassi P., C. Picanyol, W. Knechtel, M. D'Alimonte, A. Gary, A. Pomeroy-Stevens, and R. Watts. 2020. "Budget Analysis for Nutrition: Guidance Note for Countries (Update 2020)." Scaling Up Nutrition, Geneva.

Horton, S., M. Shekar, C. McDonald, A. Mahal, and J. Krystene Brooks. 2010. *Scaling Up Nutrition: What Will It Cost?* Directions in Development. Washington, DC: World Bank.

MQSUN+ (Maximising the Quality of Scaling Up Nutrition Plus). 2020. "Supplemental Guidance for the SUN Budget Analysis: An Update for Countries (Feb. 2020)." MQSUN+, Washington, DC. https://mqsunplus.path.org/resources/supplemental-guidance-for-the-sun-budget-analysis/.

Piatti-Fünfkirchen, M., L. Liang, J. K. Akuoku, and P. Mwitende. 2020. "Rwanda Nutrition Expenditure and Institutional Review." World Bank, Washington, DC.

Pradhan, S. 1996. *Evaluating Public Spending: A Framework for Public Expenditure Reviews*. World Bank Discussion Paper 323. Washington, DC: World Bank.

Shekar, M., J. Kakietek, J. Eberwein, and D. Walters. 2017. *An Investment Framework for Nutrition: Reaching the Global Targets for Stunting, Anemia, Breastfeeding, and Wasting*. Directions in Development—Human Development. Washington, DC: World Bank.

Tanzania, MoFP (Ministry of Finance and Planning) and UNICEF (United Nations Children's Fund). 2018. "Nutrition Public Expenditure Review 2014–2016: Mainland Tanzania." MoFP and UNICEF, Dar es Salaam.

World Bank. 2019. "Assessing Public Financing for Nutrition in Nepal." Unpublished report.

World Bank. 2020a. "Spending Better to Reduce Stunting in Indonesia: Findings from a Public Expenditure Review." World Bank, Washington, DC.

World Bank. 2020b. "Sri Lanka PER for Nutrition in Sri Lanka: Assessing Public Financing for Nutrition in Sri Lanka (2014–2018)." World Bank, Washington DC.

Preparation Phase

DEFINING THE SCOPE

When preparing a nutrition public expenditure review (NPER), the first step is to decide on the breadth (sector and government level) and depth (level of analytical detail) of the analysis. In terms of the breadth, the NPER should cover not only the sectors that currently have expenditure programs that address nutrition (for example, health, food and agriculture, and water and sanitation) but also the government levels that execute these programs (figure 2.1). In terms of the depth, the conceptual structure of NPERs (as presented in figure O.1) should be referenced to determine the coverage of each block within the conceptual structure. Inclusion or exclusion of particular topics should depend on numerous factors, including the (1) objectives of the NPER, as determined by the entire NPER team (What questions is the NPER trying to answer?); (2) policy priorities, as articulated in the country's nutrition strategy; (3) budget available to the NPER team; (4) time frame for the analysis; and (5) availability of data and related analytical studies to support the NPER.

When deciding on the breadth of the NPER, it is also important to consider whether it should include off-budget expenditures that do not appear in official public expenditure data.[1] In the context of nutrition, there may be off-budget programs funded by multilateral or bilateral development agencies, nongovernmental organizations (NGOs), or private companies. This type of external funding is not recorded in the national budget. Therefore, the determination of whether to include it in the NPER (and, if so, what to include and exclude) depends primarily on the scale and importance of the development programs, as well as on the available access to data or willingness to engage in primary data collection (for example, through surveys). If the NPER team determines that externally funded programs constitute a fairly large portion of the country's nutrition expenditures, there is a strong rationale for their inclusion. Several NPERs have included expenditures from development partners, including Bangladesh, Rwanda, and Tanzania.

A public expenditure review (PER) typically limits its scope to the expenditure side of public finance and does not examine the revenue side. A program focused on the revenue side of nutrition could refer, for example, to certain taxes

FIGURE 2.1
Nutrition activities span different government levels and multiple line ministries

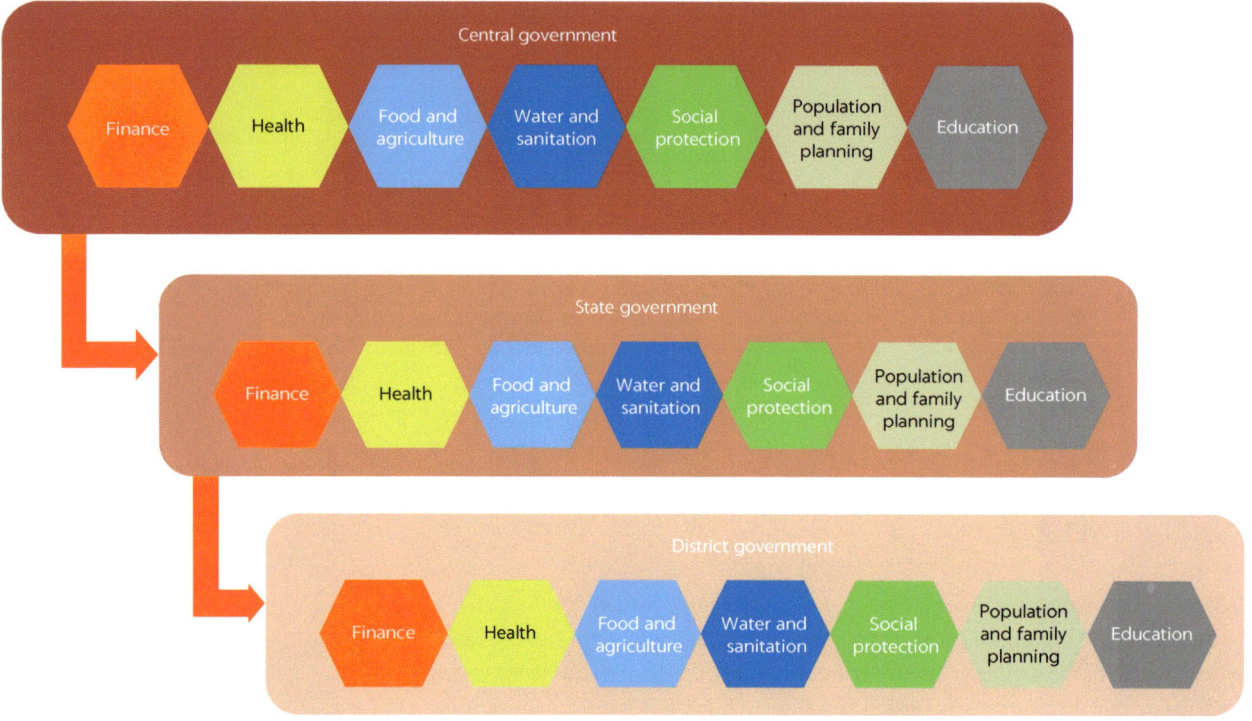

Source: World Bank.

that may have a large impact on nutrition, such as taxation for sugar-sweetened beverages, which more than 40 countries had adopted as of March 2019 (Shekar and Popkin 2020). In some countries, certain tax policies could have a significant impact on nutrition outcomes by affecting people's behavior in ways that affect nutrition, such as the consumption pattern of unhealthy foods and drinks. Therefore, although an examination of the revenue side is usually not part of a PER, an NPER team could potentially consider including such non-expenditure-related policies in future NPERs if such policies are expected to have an overbearing influence on nutrition outcomes or on the effectiveness or efficiency of their existing nutrition expenditure programs.[2]

NPERs can also be used to assess elements of existing major nutrition-related expenditure policies. PERs that focus on specific sectors, such as agriculture, often directly address such major expenditure policies with the intent to influence dialogue on policy reform for existing legacy programs; however, this area has not been explored in the existing set of NPERs. For example, NPERs could assess large-scale supplementary feeding (that is, fortified food) programs, because these programs often consume the bulk (or majority) of nutrition spending but are highly political and based on weak evidence, prone to leakage, and often unsustainable. Thus, NPERs could be useful in efforts to understand the efficiency of spending, which could inform future policy dialogues.

In terms of depth of the analysis, the team must decide on the choice of analysis to determine the effectiveness, efficiency, or equity of nutrition expenditures. Unlike sector PERs, no existing NEPR has been able to carry out an effectiveness or technical efficiency analysis. In the preparation phase, the team needs to study the available data, assess the quality of those data, and decide on which analysis to carry out. The NPER should clearly indicate why certain key analyses are omitted, and it could supplement any omission with qualitative assessments. NPERs can also help identify and make concrete recommendations on critical data gaps that need to be addressed to answer key performance and accountability questions.

ESTABLISHING AN NPER TEAM

The purpose of an NPER is to help policy makers make better policy, planning, and budgetary decisions. Without government engagement, the NPER will be a stand-alone research exercise that does not serve its main objective of influencing policy to achieve better results. It is, therefore, important that the NPER team consist of members of the government and technical or financial organizations, so that all parties are actively involved and assume ownership of the NPER and its recommendations and conclusions.

The NPER team should decide on the main government entity to engage according to the intended purpose of the NPER. The main government entity is often (1) the agency that chairs the existing national nutrition coordination body, which has the mandate to coordinate government efforts to improve nutrition; (2) the ministry of finance or planning; or (3) the ministry of health, with the active participation of other ministries, depending on the demand, the intended purpose, and data requirements (box 2.1). If the issues to be addressed require actions by specific government ministries, these authorities should be engaged in the NPER process. For example:

- Public financial management issues related to spending levels, the overall budget cycle, budget releases, and accountability usually require actions by the ministry of finance.
- Issues related to decentralization, including fiscal transfers, usually require actions by the ministry of local government.
- Issues on the composition of spending usually require actions by the line ministry(ies), such as health, agriculture, or social welfare.

BOX 2.1

Lead government entities involved in existing nutrition public expenditure reviews

- *Bangladesh:* Finance Division, Ministry of Finance
- *Bhutan:* Ministry of Health, Ministry of Agriculture and Forests
- *Indonesia:* Vice President's Office, which heads the oversight body of the multisectoral nutrition program
- *Nepal:* National Planning Commission
- *Rwanda:* National Early Childhood Development Program, which coordinates all nutrition activities
- *Sri Lanka:* Nutrition Technical Working Group, chaired by the Department of National Planning, with members from the Presidential Secretariat
- *Tanzania:* Prime Minister's Office

The role of each member of the NPER team needs to be clear. The team needs to decide on the competencies of staff and consultants from technical or financial organizations. A nutrition specialist leading this effort on behalf of the organization may want to recruit staff or a consultant with complementary skills such as public financial management. Practitioners from government entities can have varying roles, from leading the entire process to being part of the preparation team, and they can be updated throughout the process or engaged at the beginning and end of it. The team will need to weigh the benefits and costs of proposed NPER team structures and assess trade-offs. The team should consider the following:

- Ensuring that government entities are part of the preparation team, which may help to obtain easier access to public expenditure data. Public officials can facilitate access to information from different government sources and aid in the interpretation of the NPER.
- Engaging senior government officials at various stages of preparation to speed up the adoption of recommendations.
- Involving a large group of technical experts in the analytical process, which could enhance the rigorousness of the exercise but would likely add to the cost and time required to complete it. To ensure the uptake of recommendations, the team could encourage broad stakeholder engagement by adopting a participatory process and plan (at least during the planning and dissemination and follow-on dialogue stages) that include platforms to facilitate a dialogue across sectors.

PREPARING A WORK PLAN

Best practices suggest preparing a work plan that covers the areas addressed in this preparatory phase as well as any country-specific issues and including administrative elements such as budget, time frame, and team composition. This plan can be used to form a common understanding between all parties of the NPER team, including government entities, to ensure there are no misunderstandings. A well-researched work plan should facilitate the actual drafting of the NPER and clarify agreed-on objectives, concepts, and scope. Although each work plan should be customized to satisfy the requirements of the funding organization (or other stakeholders), common elements include the following:

- Context
- Government request (if applicable)
- Objectives and audience
- Synthesis of recent literature, link to past and ongoing activities, and value addition of the proposed NPER
- Scope and methodology of the study
- Consultation plan with key stakeholders
- Dissemination plan
- Resources/budget
- Team composition of technical agency staff or consultants and government officials (with expertise identified), potentially including experts from outside the nutrition field, such as those from public sector management or agriculture

- Timetable
- Technical review (or quality control) process, such as composition of a technical advisory group or names of individual peer reviewers
- Key annexes, such as a draft outline of the report, a brief overview of the nutrition context (main trends and issues), and a list of key references

IDENTIFYING DATA SOURCES

Broadly, two types of data are needed for an NPER: (1) data on nutrition financing to quantify nutrition expenditures, and (2) data on performance indicators to understand the impact of financial investments. The main source of financing data is the country's financial management information system (FMIS) or other complementary data sources. Potential sources of performance data include population-based surveys and program administrative records. If the quality of the financing data is poor, the NPER team may need to undertake small sample surveys and highlight efforts to improve data quality in the recommendation section of the NPER.

Data sources for nutrition financing

A comprehensive data set on nutrition financing should do the following:

- Cover budget allocation, execution, and realized spending across all sectors that deliver nutrition-specific and nutrition-sensitive interventions. Such data should be over at least a few years to ensure that the analysis is not dominated by any single-year anomalies.
- Capture the flow of funds (including identification of fund holders at different levels), financing sources, and the economic classification of spending (for example, salaries, goods and services, and capital expenses).
- Disaggregate spending across all government levels (that is, national, regional, and subregional).
- Present a programmatic classification for each budget line item.

A general starting point for collecting nutrition financing data is the country's audited official budget data system managed by the ministry of finance. Many countries provide this information through an FMIS that records budget formulation, execution (for example, commitment control, cash/debt management, and treasury operations), accounting, and reporting. Some countries have automated and integrated the FMIS, and the budget is recorded in an integrated FMIS (IFMIS) platform.[3] The automated nature of an IFMIS allows the authorities to access readily available, timely, and accurate information; this ability is critical to the management of government finances and public funds, which are characterized by large transaction volumes and data dispersal across multiple sites around the country (Hashim 2014). Some countries participate in the BOOST initiative, which offers a tool to better use the FMIS/IFMIS data by improving the organization and analysis of data in a user-friendly format.[4] The ministry of finance often keeps detailed records of expenditure data for different ministries and levels of government, although the level of data available varies across countries. The level of disaggregation needed for an NPER will most likely require access to subnational data, not only at the provincial level but possibly also at the district and local levels.

Complementary data sources can be used to supplement government data. Potential complementary data include the following:

- *National Health Accounts (NHA) data.* The World Health Organization's NHA tracks spending that flows through the health sector.[5] Nutrition expenditures are captured mainly within the nutrition deficiencies category—one of the five spending categories tracked by the NHA. The NHA, however, is unlikely to capture nutrition-relevant financing for programs related to disease prevention and control, maternal care, and noncommunicable diseases, among others. Because the NHA primarily targets financing only in the health sector, relying entirely on the NHA data set will lead to underestimating nutrition-related spending. Nevertheless, NHA information could fill gaps in domestic data reporting in the health sector.
- *Insurance claims data.* Data from insurance agencies can be relevant for the NPER analysis in countries where insurance programs make up a significant share of nutrition financing, particularly for expenditures on nutrition-specific interventions and some nutrition-sensitive interventions such as maternal and child service. Specifically, insurance records (for example, information on claims, patient management records, and so on) that can provide detailed information on interventions received could be useful for identifying nutrition-related expenditures.[6] Moreover, as a further potential use, insurance claims data could demonstrate the effectiveness of nutrition spending through an examination of spending on medical care that could have been avoided with better nutrition programs (there are no examples of such analyses carried out to date in NPERs).
- *Off-budget development partner data.* In many countries where a significant part of the health sector is financed by bilateral and multilateral development partners, off-budget funding is reported in separate data sets such as the Aid Information Management System,[7] the Aid Management Platform,[8] and the Organisation for Economic Co-operation and Development's Creditor Reporting System.[9] Among these data sets, the Aid Information Management System or Aid Management Platform is recommended because each is considered of sufficiently high quality, whereas the Creditor Reporting System, which is based on voluntary reporting at an aggregated level, is recommended only when the other two are unavailable. When multiple off-budget data sources are available, the NPER team should consider using only one database to curb the risk of double counting, but the decision should be made by considering the completeness and quality of available data. A country can also use one database and validate off-budget information with data from the next available source, as has been done in the Bangladesh NPER for development partner funding to NGOs and foundations (box 2.2). In countries where none of these data sources are available, the team would need to collect primary data, as has been done in the case of the Rwanda NPER. The Global Financing Facility, a multistakeholder global partnership housed in the World Bank, has developed the Resource Mapping and Expenditure Tracking tool for this purpose, which can be used to collate development partner data.[10]

Data sources for nutrition results

The goal of nutrition financing is to improve nutrition results. Thus, the NPER team needs to identify data sources for nutrition performance indicators, based

> **BOX 2.2**
>
> ### Experience from the Bangladesh NPER on estimating donor funding for nutrition investments implemented by nongovernmental organizations
>
> In Bangladesh, the nutrition public expenditure review (NPER) team hypothesized that a significant amount of investment for nutrition comes from outside of the government system through activities implemented by nongovernmental organizations and funded by donors. To estimate the size of such investments, the Bangladesh NPER used multiple databases: the Country Investment Plan Development Partners sheet, the Aid Information Management System under the Economic Relations Division of the Ministry of Finance, and the Organisation for Economic Co-operation and Development's Creditor Reporting System, all of which captured donor funding to nongovernmental organizations. The Organisation for Economic Co-operation and Development's Creditor Reporting System databases were screened first by relevant thematic areas (nutrition; health; water, sanitation, and hygiene; social protection; livelihoods; education; and agriculture) and then by a keyword search to identify relevant projects and programs.
>
> The information in the Creditor Reporting System database was more limited and therefore was used only for triangulation of the information found in the Aid Information Management System and in the Country Investment Plan Development Partners sheet. From the list of projects and programs identified through the keyword search, some were dropped because they were deemed not relevant. For those projects and programs that were unclear in terms of their nutrition relevance, the NPER undertook a search of project and program websites, donor and implementing organization websites, and available project documents to determine inclusion or exclusion. After some final adjustments on the implementation time period of the projects and programs, the NPER estimated that nutrition investments implemented by nongovernmental organizations and funded by donors amounted to approximately US$736 million over three years, which was approximately 10 percent of the total government expenditures on nutrition during that time.
>
> *Source:* Finance Division, Government of the Republic of Bangladesh and UNICEF 2019.

primarily on the output, outcome, or impact levels of the results framework (or log frame) of the national nutrition plan or strategy.[11]

The NPER team may need to access multiple data sources for performance indicators on the national and subnational levels. When data sources overlap, the NPER team should determine the most accurate source of information in cooperation with the main government entity. Potential data sources include the following:

- *Nationally or regionally representative household surveys.* Such surveys are the most likely sources of both impact data and other monitoring and evaluation indicators. The most frequently used surveys are the Demographic and Health Surveys (DHS) and the Multiple Indicator Cluster Surveys (MICS), which include a range of population, health, nutrition, and socioeconomic indicators that are standardized across countries. The DHS and MICS are usually updated every 5 or 10 years. Additionally, some countries conduct nutrition-focused SMART surveys to provide data between the DHS and MICS, although these surveys are usually done only in countries suffering from fragility, conflict, and violence.[12] Aside from the DHS and MICS, countries may conduct other nationally representative household

surveys. For example, the Basic Health Research (Riset Kesehatan Dasar, RISKESDAS) household survey in Indonesia provided the Indonesia NPER team with information on nutrition-related output, intermediate outcome, and final outcome indicators.
- *Program administrative data* generated as a part of a program's operations could be useful for output and intermediate outcome indicators. Data quality may, however, vary across countries and programs, and indicators need to be carefully interpreted. Data could be vetted by comparing indicators from different sources, and data quality could be assessed through consultations with project staff on the process of collecting and recording data. The NPER team should also check if the country uses DHIS2 (District Health Information Software), a health information management system platform that collects aggregated data on routine services at health facilities, staffing, equipment, and infrastructure, among other variables. DHIS2 covers both input and output indicators and can provide insights into how the quality of nutrition-related data is addressed.[13]

In some countries, the government already uses a system like a country performance monitoring dashboard, which integrates financial and sector performance data into one data set. This system contrasts with the more common case, in which financial and sector performance data are recorded in separate databases. As it relates to nutrition, this practice implies a dashboard on which expenditures on nutrition and some key nutrition performance outcomes are displayed side by side in one system. Such a system is not commonly found in most developing countries but is best practice in terms of understanding the link between financing and the corresponding outcomes. For example, a recent reform in Indonesia focuses on connecting various financial and performance monitoring data systems to make it easier to share and analyze information. The Ministry of Finance's OM-SPAN (Online Monitoring System of the Financial Management Information System), which provides information on budget allocation and execution, has been connected to an online integrated performance monitoring application called SMART, which in turn records output data on each work unit in the ministry or agency using OM-SPAN. Thus, information on budget realization and results at the output level are simultaneously accessible to track spending and outputs, enabling stock taking and quick evaluation by line ministries.

NOTES

1. Unlike some health sector public expenditure reviews, existing NPERs do not include household expenditures because of the lack of available data.
2. No NPER to date includes such an analysis.
3. When FMIS and other public financial management information systems (for example, e-procurement, payroll, and debt management) are linked with a central data warehouse to record and report all daily financial transactions offering reliable consolidated platforms, this system can be referred to as an integrated FMIS (IFMIS). Broadly, an IFMIS consists of a set of computer programs, databases, associated processes, procedures, and technology platforms that enable government finance and accounting staff to carry out their day-to-day operational tasks.
4. Launched in 2010, the World Bank's BOOST program has active engagements in over 90 developing countries to provide high-quality access to budget data. The initiative strives to make well-classified and highly disaggregated budget data available to governments,

5. practitioners, researchers, and civil society and promotes their effective use for improved budgetary decision-making, analysis, transparency, and accountability. The appeal of the BOOST approach is that it provides user-friendly platforms on which all expenditure data can be easily accessed and used to examine trends in allocations of public resources as well as to analyze potential sources of inefficiencies so that citizens can become better informed about how governments finance the delivery of public services. More details can be found on the BOOST Open Budget Portal (https://www.worldbank.org/en/programs/boost-portal/about-boost).
5. The NHA includes data on public, private, and donor health expenditures, although countries, especially low- and middle-income countries, may not update their data sets regularly. Price et al. (2016) report that only 41 countries, overwhelmingly Organisation for Economic Co-operation and Development member countries, provide regular updates to the NHA.
6. Obviously, the usefulness of these data sources depends on the payment mechanisms and the level of record completeness. A fee-for-service system may be more straightforward than a capitation system, especially when the capitation is not accompanied by pseudo-billing. In general, most of the information can be found from insurance records related to ambulatory visits, but the team needs to consider the pattern of service delivery use.
7. See the International Aid Transparency Initiative web page on Aid Information Management Systems (https://iatistandard.org/en/iati-tools-and-resources/aims/).
8. For a general description, see the Development Gateway web page on aid management (https://developmentgateway.org/expertise/aid-management/). For a list of countries and the URLs of their respective Aid Management Platforms, see annex F of Fracassi et al. (2020).
9. See the Creditor Reporting System database (https://stats.oecd.org/Index.aspx?DataSetCode=crs1).
10. For more information, see the Global Financing Facility's Resource Library (https://www.globalfinancingfacility.org/resource-mapping-and-expenditure-tracking-lessons-learned-countries).
11. If the national nutrition plan or strategy does not include a results framework (or log frame), the NPER team will need to discuss and agree on what the specific outputs, outcomes, and impacts are according to a reading of the nutrition plan or strategy.
12. SMART surveys are recognized as the standard methodology by national ministries of health, donors, and implementing partners of the Global Nutrition Cluster, such as international NGOs and United Nations agencies that wish to undertake nutrition and mortality surveys. The Global Nutrition Cluster is a group of 33 members from various NGOs involved in nutrition; it meets regularly to exchange information on nutrition emergencies at the global level. With the United Nations Children's Fund (UNICEF) as the lead agency, the Global Nutrition Cluster develops open access to institutional archives and resources for cluster implementation in a user-friendly manner (https://smartmethodology.org/about-smart/).
13. See the DHIS2 Documentation web page (https://docs.dhis2.org/en/home.html).

REFERENCES

Finance Division, Government of the Republic of Bangladesh and UNICEF (United Nations Children's Fund), 2019. *Bangladesh Public Expenditure Review on Nutrition*. Dhaka: Government of Bangladesh and UNICEF.

Fracassi P., C. Picanyol, W. Knechtel, M. D'Alimonte, A. Gary, A. Pomeroy-Stevens, and R. Watts. 2020. "Budget Analysis for Nutrition: Guidance Note for Countries (Update 2020)." Scaling Up Nutrition, Geneva.

Hashim, A. 2014. "A Handbook on Financial Management Information Systems for Government: A Practitioners Guide for Setting Reform Priorities, Systems Design, and Implementation." Africa Operations Services Series, World Bank, Washington, DC. https://documents1.worldbank.org/curated/en/147241467987856662/pdf/A-handbook-on-financial-management-information-systems-for-government-a-practitioners-guide-for-setting-reform-priorities-systems-design-and-implementation.pdf.

Price, J., L. Guinness, W. Irava, I. Khan, A. Asante, and V. Wiseman. 2016. "How to Do (or Not to Do) . . . Translation of National Health Accounts Data to Evidence for Policy Making in a Low Resourced Setting." *Health Policy and Planning* 31 (4): 472–81.

Shekar, M., and B. Popkin. 2020. *Obesity: Health and Economic Consequences of an Impending Global Challenge*. Human Development Perspectives. Washington, DC: World Bank.

Key Elements of an NPER

This chapter presents key elements that are recommended to be covered in a nutrition public expenditure review (NPER). The headings of this chapter can be considered a skeleton outline of an NPER:

- (Introduction)
- Country context
- National nutrition strategy
- Institutional framework and budget process
- Identifying nutrition expenditures
- Analysis
  - Expenditure levels and trends
  - Composition of expenditures
  - Service coverage and utilization
  - Effectiveness
  - Efficiency
    - Allocative efficiency
    - Technical efficiency
    - Administrative efficiency
  - Equity
- (Conclusion, recommendations, moving forward)

COUNTRY CONTEXT

To understand the country context, the NPER team needs to present key economic and health indicators (and their links to nutrition outcomes) as well as nutrition indicators. It also needs to describe how these have changed over time and how they compare with those of peer countries. Relevant metrics to present include the following:

- *Economic indicators.* Poverty rate, per capita gross national income or gross domestic product, annual gross national income/gross domestic product growth rate, population, population growth rate, human capital index, shared prosperity indicators, size of government spending, government revenues, and debt

- *Health indicators.* Per capita health expenditures; life expectancy at birth; fertility; under-five, infant, and maternal mortality rates; and disease burden (top-10 causes of death and disability, top-10 risk factors causing death and disability)[1]
- *Nutrition indicators.*[2] Under-five stunting, reproductive-age female anemia rate, low birth weight, under-five overweight, exclusive breastfeeding up to six months, and childhood wasting.

Comparisons with regional peers or appropriate benchmarks (for example, regional average, global average, and countries at similar income levels) put the country's health and nutrition statistics in perspective. Benchmarks that compare a country's metrics with those of relevant peer countries can be a simple yet powerful way of highlighting spending inefficiency that often resonates with policy makers. For example, Indonesia successfully decreased early childhood mortality from 97 to 32 deaths per 1,000 live births between 1990 and 2017. However, its stunting rates remain among the highest in the world (27.7 percent in 2019) and much higher than those of other countries of similar income levels, such as Sri Lanka (13 percent; figure 3.1).

The NPER should also reveal any within-country disparities. Such data can highlight geographical areas with the highest need (or areas that are most in need of nutrition interventions), provide guidance on what kind of analysis the NPER should undertake, and feed into policy recommendations for strategies to reach the last mile or inform fiscal transfer strategies to reduce disparities. For instance, the Bhutan NPER shows that stunting rates are higher in eastern Bhutan and rural areas and that the prevalence of stunting among households in the poorest income quintile (35 percent) is markedly higher than among households in the richest quintile (5 percent; figure 3.2).

FIGURE 3.1

Example from the Indonesia NPER: Stunting rate relative to comparators

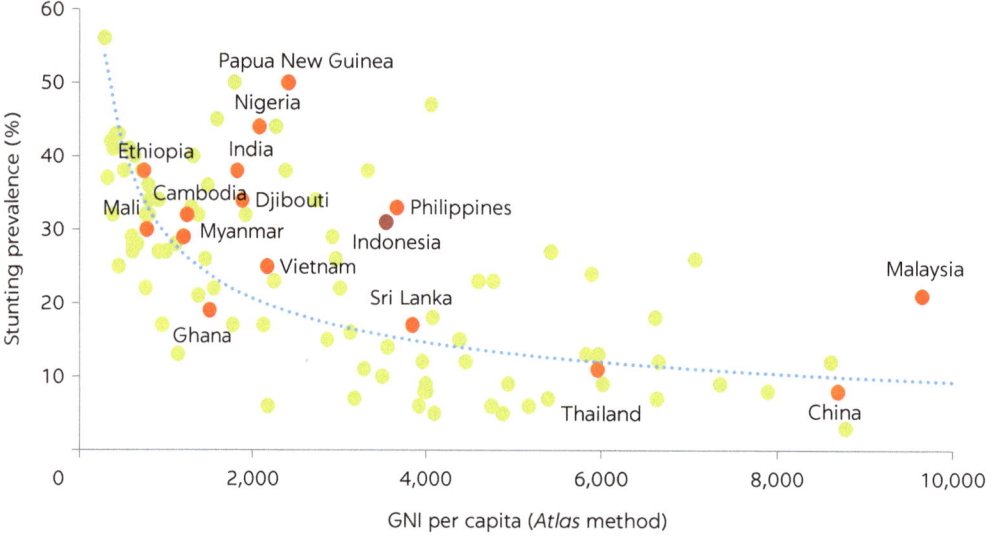

Sources: World Bank 2020a; Word Development Indicators data for 2019; data for Indonesia from the Basic Health Research (Riset Kesehatan Dasar, RISKESDAS) survey 2018.
Note: Stunting prevalence of children under five years of age. The World Bank uses the *Atlas* conversion factor instead of simple exchange rates. The purpose of the *Atlas* conversion factor is to reduce the impact of exchange rate fluctuations in the cross-country comparison of national incomes. The *Atlas* conversion factor for any year is the average of a country's exchange rate for that year and its exchange rates for the two preceding years, adjusted for the difference between the rate of inflation in the country and international inflation.
GNI = gross national income; NPER = nutrition public expenditure review.

FIGURE 3.2

Example from the Bhutan NPER: Stunting by region, area, age, and wealth

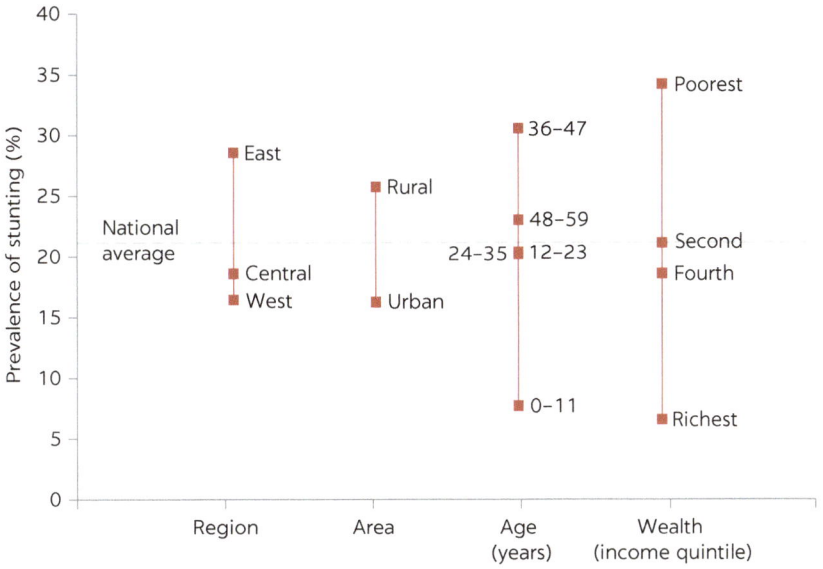

Source: Ahmed et al. 2020.
Note: Dashed line in figure shows the national average (21.2 percent). NPER = nutrition public expenditure review.

NATIONAL NUTRITION STRATEGY

NPERs should be guided first and foremost by the country's nutrition strategy. The national nutrition strategy relates to NPERs in two main ways. First, NPERs should present a clear view of the country nutrition strategy to set the context, although this task may not be simple or straightforward in countries that have multiple strategies that address nutrition, each with its own set of identified priorities that are not necessarily coherent. Second, the priorities of the country's nutrition strategy should determine key areas of the NPER, from the scope of work to the types of analyses that will be carried out. Specifically, NPERs should try to assess whether nutrition financing levels and trends have been consistent with priorities identified in the nutrition strategy and whether, with the existing nutrition financing, results envisioned in the country nutrition strategy have been achieved (or not).

NPERs should clearly present the country's nutrition strategy and specific objectives. Anchoring the NPER to the country's policy framework would make it more relevant to policy makers and help them meet their policy commitments (box 3.1). For example, a country's primary nutrition goal may be to reduce stunting due to malnutrition, or it may be to address all three dimensions of malnutrition (undernutrition, micronutrient deficiency, and overweight and obesity).[3] However, less ideal situations could exist, such as when countries do not have a national nutrition policy, the nutrition strategy is not a stand-alone strategy and is instead a part of health sector priorities, or the nutrition strategy has a very limited scope. In these scenarios, the NPER team needs to agree with the government on what the country's nutrition objectives are before embarking on the NPER.

> **BOX 3.1**
>
> ### How NPERs are aligned with national nutrition policy goals
>
> The Bhutan nutrition public expenditure review (NPER) is aligned with the Food and Nutrition Security policy document, which outlines the country's nutrition strategy. Bhutan prioritizes efforts to reduce micronutrient deficiencies and improve nutrition among adolescent girls, children under the age of five, women of reproductive age, and pregnant and lactating women.
>
> The Indonesia NPER focuses on stunting because the country's authorities view human capital as one of the key pillars for achieving Indonesia's 2045 vision. Reducing stunting is an essential component of human capital, and Indonesia's stunting rates are among the highest in the world.
>
> In Rwanda, the NPER is aligned with the objectives of the National Early Childhood Development Program Strategic Plan, which coordinates all interventions that support early childhood development from conception to six years of age. It is characterized by eight strategic directions aimed at increasing the coverage and quality of high-impact, evidence-based integrated early childhood development interventions. The fact that the information on outcomes and expenditures is not regularly published and its activities are not costed out in the strategic plan creates challenges for its successful implementation.

NPERs should assess the clarity, alignment, and appropriateness of nutrition strategies and goals. Questions to address include the following:

- Are the country's nutrition goals clearly stated and supported by clearly articulated strategies or action plans? If the country has subnational nutrition strategies or plans, are they aligned with national strategies and plans?
- Are the goals broadly aligned with the framework for actions to achieve optimum fetal and child nutrition and development, as published in *The Lancet* (the "*Lancet* framework"; see appendix A)?
- Are priorities evidence-based and aligned with global recommendations for high-impact interventions?
- Do different strategies complement each other, or are they contradictory?
- Are institutional arrangements clearly presented, with roles and responsibilities for different agencies?
- Are goals supported by tangible results indicators, target values, and clear timelines (to achieve the targets)? Is there a process for measuring progress?
- Are interventions costed out so that identified priority interventions are not just a wish list?

INSTITUTIONAL FRAMEWORK AND BUDGET PROCESS

> Indicative questions that the NPER could address:
>
> - *What are the characteristics of the institutional framework for addressing nutrition in the country (including any nutrition coordination mechanisms)?*

- *What are the key delivery platforms across sectors and levels of government?*
- *How does financing flow (including to decentralized levels of government and various delivery platforms)?*
- *What are the government planning and budget management systems that are applicable to multisectoral policy and plans?*

The NPER needs to describe and assess the country's institutional framework for addressing nutrition. Many countries have established an interministerial nutrition coordination mechanism that drives the coordination of interventions included in the country's nutrition strategy. These mechanisms can be chaired by the prime minister, vice president, minister of health, or head of another government agency. The NPER should describe its specific mandates and roles, and assess the strength and how the mechanism is carrying out its mandate. The NPER should discuss the overall effectiveness of the nutrition coordination mechanism, including (1) whether it plays any role (or has the potential to play such a role in the future) in the national budget process that combines a top-down, whole-of-government policy framework, led by central finance and planning agencies, with a bottom-up process of expenditure planning by spending agencies; (2) its tools to hold stakeholders accountable; (3) its ability to follow up on whether budgets have been released, understand what activities have been implemented, and monitor cash flow issues across implementing agencies; and (4) whether the legislative branch is engaged in the process.[4]

In terms of the budget process, public expenditure reviews (PERs) typically present a step-by-step annual budget process diagram or fund flow diagram to show how financing flows to beneficiaries. The annual budget process diagram of a given country would show how the central finance and planning agencies initiate the budget process, usually six to nine months before the start of the fiscal year. It would typically do so by preparing a pre-budget policy document that lays out the macroeconomic framework and proposes the broad allocation of resources in line with government plans and policies. This is followed by numerous steps, such as the issuing of budget circulars and ceilings, the preparation of budget proposals by spending agencies, negotiations with central financing and planning agencies, budget approval processes involving parliamentary approval, the release of funds, reporting on budget use, and finally an independent audit of final accounts after the fiscal year. The fund flow diagram highlights where the funds originate, the authorities that administer them, and where they are finally spent. The schematic of the financing flows can help the NPER team organize and focus the analysis by identifying key financiers and government authorities involved in nutrition-related expenditures. Figure 3.3 provides an example of the budget process diagram from the Tanzania NPER.

Given the multisectoral nature of nutrition programs, NPERs may include an assessment of how the current public financial management (PFM) system coordinates nutrition expenditures across sectors and levels of government. Multisectoral nutrition programs involve several government agencies, programs, and subprograms that require PFM mechanisms to guide the planning and budgeting phase to ensure that nutrition-related activities of all agencies are

FIGURE 3.3
Example from the Tanzania NPER: Budget process diagram

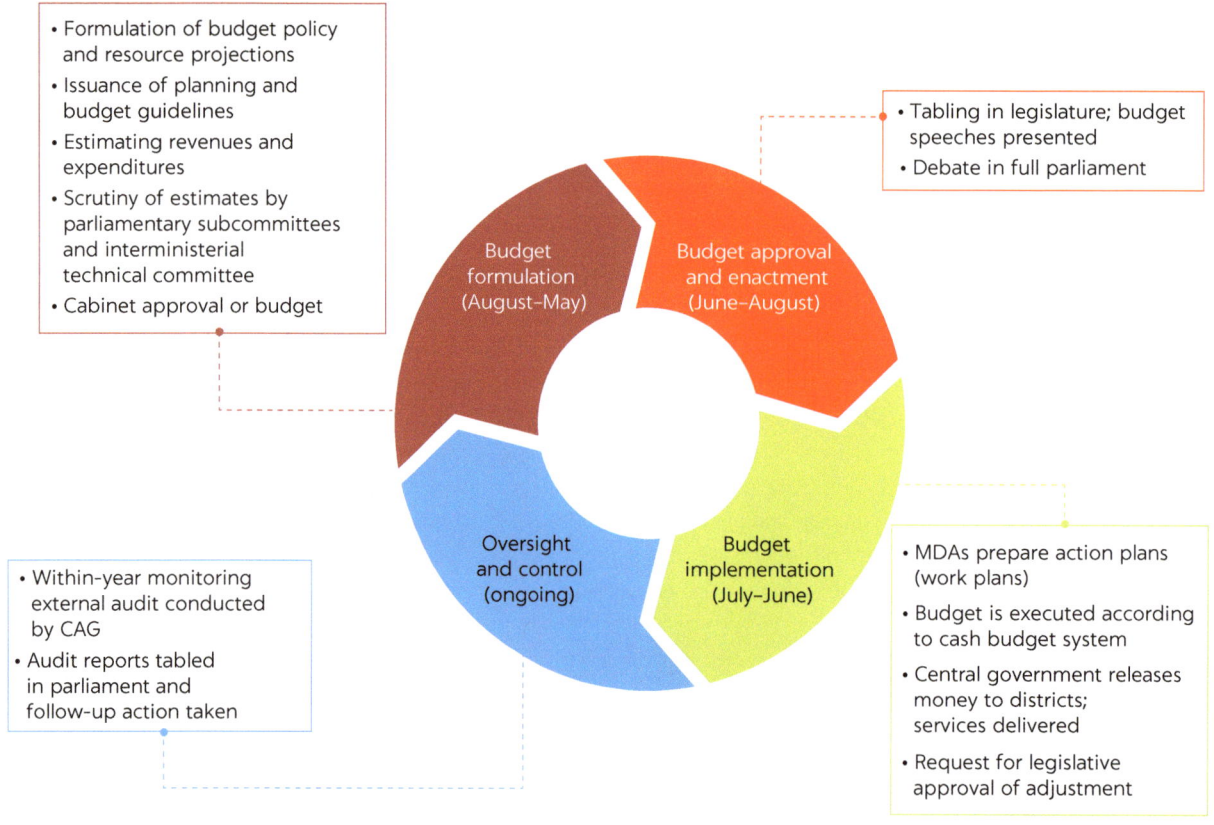

Source: Tanzania, MoFP and UNICEF 2018.
Note: CAG = Controller and Auditor General; MDAs = ministries, departments, and agencies; NPER = nutrition public expenditure review.

prioritized and aligned with the national nutrition policy. The NPER team can conduct an assessment of how current PFM systems work to manage the budget formulation process and monitor budget releases across all agencies against appropriations. In Indonesia and Rwanda, detailed discussions on the PFM process helped the analysis and formulation of recommendations to improve the quality and availability of financing data.

Because nutrition-related activities are multisectoral, there are likely many implementing agencies and delivery platforms involved in executing nutrition expenditures. The NPER team should identify the country's prevailing delivery channels for a variety of nutrition services. Nutrition-specific interventions are usually delivered through health service delivery platforms, and many nutrition services are already integrated into health care delivery systems. However, in many countries some nutrition services are delivered outside the formal health sector (for example, through community-level platforms outside the public health system). Furthermore, nutrition-sensitive interventions are delivered through other delivery platforms, such as schools, to reach the intended target group (for example, adolescent girls). Hence, it would be helpful to explain the different delivery platforms involved. For example, the Rwanda NPER shows that financing for nutrition-sensitive activities is channeled through 29 programs and 54 subprograms. Indonesia, by contrast, has three main delivery platforms: village health posts, village water and sanitation organizations, and village playgroups (figure 3.4).

FIGURE 3.4
Example from the Indonesia NPER: Flow of nutrition financing

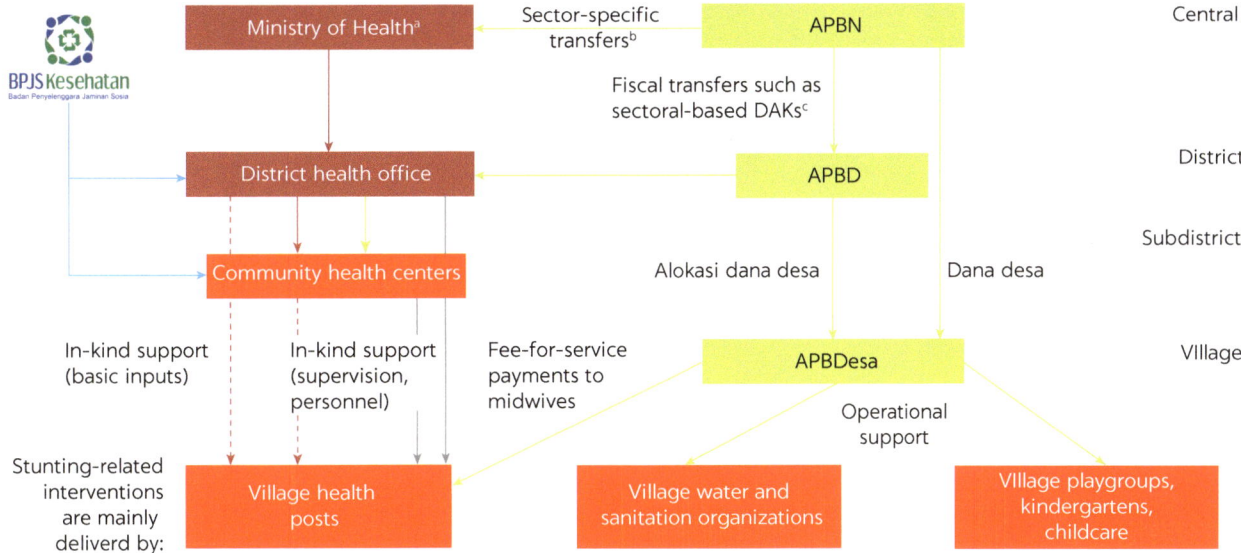

Source: World Bank 2020a.
Note: APBD = district budget; APBDesa = village budget; APBN = state budget; BPJS-Kesehatan = national health insurance agency; DAK = special allocation fund; JKN = national health insurance program; NPER = nutrition public expenditure review.
a. Nutrition-related Ministry of Health resources are fragmented across several directorates by program, disease, and level of service delivery (for example, Directorates of Family Health, Environmental Health, Public Nutrition, Health Promotion and Community Empowerment, Prevention/Control of Infectious Disease, Prevention/Control of Vector and Zoonotic Disease, Prevention/Control of Non-Communicable Disease, Management of Public Medicine and Health Supplies, Primary Health Services, and Referral Health Services).
b. For simplicity, only flows through the Ministry of Health are shown, but resources also flow from the state budget to other relevant ministries, such as Social Affairs, Education, Public Works and Housing.
c. Nutrition-related DAKs are also fragmented across sectors (11 across health, water and sanitation, education). Other transfers include Dana Bagi Hasil (DBH), Dana Alokasi Umum (DAU), and central grants—mostly used for funding salaries.

IDENTIFYING NUTRITION EXPENDITURES

Indicative questions that the NPER could address:

- *How is the level of nutrition expenditures determined?*
- *Should disaggregation weights be used in determining the level of nutrition expenditures? If so, when and how?*
- *How do we deal with high-cost, nutrition-sensitive interventions (for example, infrastructure for water pipes)? Should all of it be counted as nutrition expenditures or just some of it?*

To identify nutrition expenditure items, the NPER team should follow the seven steps outlined in the flow chart in figure 3.5. It is important to note that the use of disaggregation weights does not appear until the last step (Step 7), after a budget line item has passed the inclusion criteria filter (Step 5).

Step 1. Review country strategies or action plans to identify which programs and interventions are relevant to nutrition. It is also important for the NPER team to identify the sectors and ministries responsible for the programs and interventions.

FIGURE 3.5
Flow chart of steps to identify nutrition expenditures

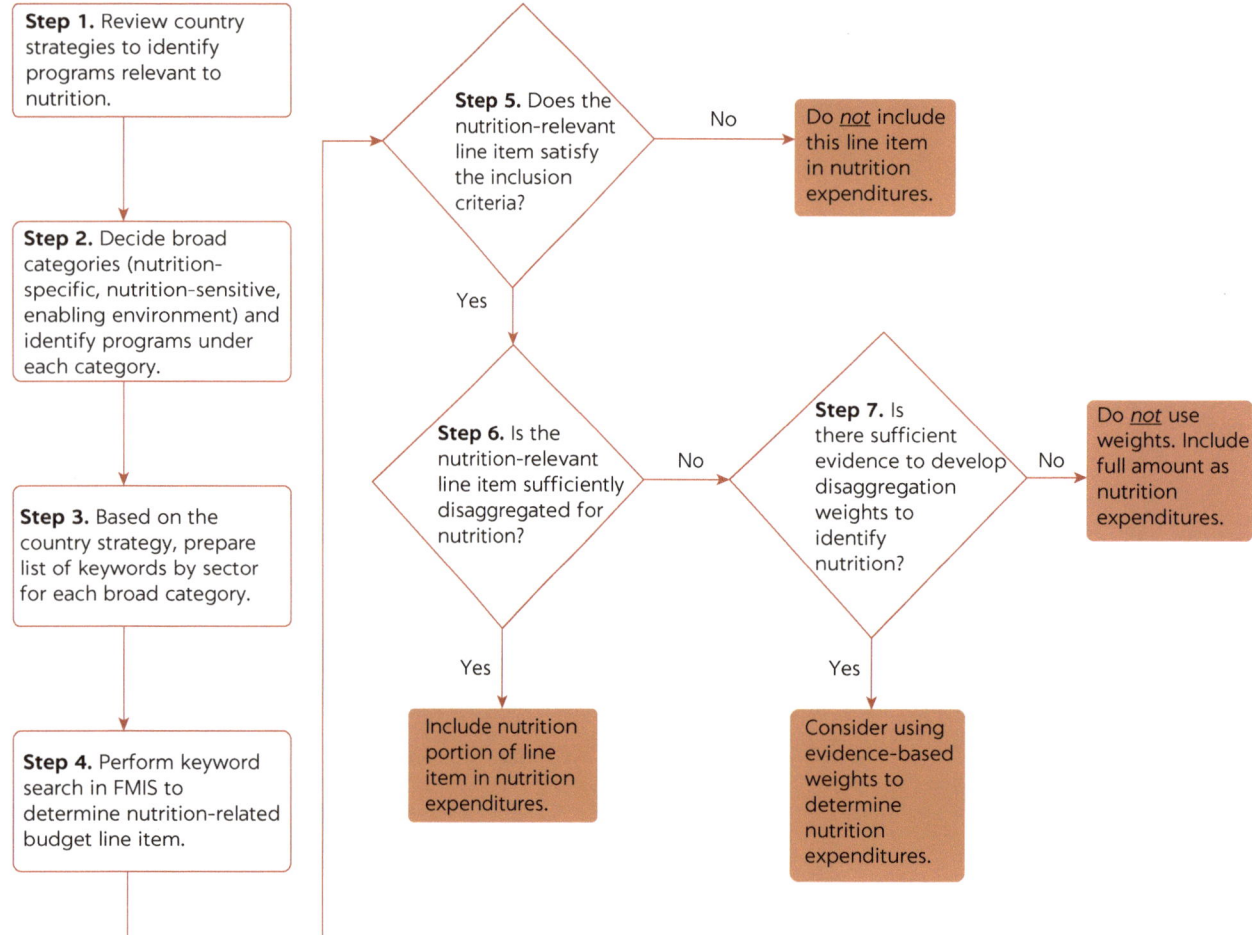

Source: World Bank.
Note: FMIS = financial management information system.

Table 3.1 includes an example of a list of identified interventions from the Indonesia NPER.

Step 2. Decide on broad categories (for example, nutrition-specific or nutrition-sensitive interventions and enabling environment), and identify programs and interventions under each category. The *Lancet* framework (appendix A) constitutes a good starting point to identify categories, because it is based on an extensive review of existing evidence. Another benefit of using the *Lancet* framework for categorization is that it allows for a comparison across countries. If a country decides to use a different method of categorization than the *Lancet* framework (for example, placing a school feeding program in the nutrition-specific category rather than in the nutrition-sensitive intervention category), it is good practice to document the justification for future reference. Table 3.2 includes a list of the interventions and programs under each nutrition category extracted from the *Lancet* framework.

Step 3. Prepare a comprehensive list of keywords by sector and ministry. An important resource to help the NPER team to develop a list of keywords for an NPER is the Scaling Up Nutrition (SUN) Budget Analysis for Nutrition, which

TABLE 3.1 Example from the Indonesia NPER: Nutrition-related interventions

	INTERVENTIONS
Nutrition-specific	• Supplementary feeding for chronic energy-deficiency in women • Iron folic acid supplementation • Exclusive breastfeeding counseling • Prenatal health checkups • Infant and young child feeding counseling • Integrated management of chronic malnutrition • Growth monitoring and promotion • Vitamin A supplementation • Micronutrient supplementation • Complete immunization • Zinc supplementation • Integrated management of child illness
Nutrition-sensitive	Water and sanitation • Access to clean water and drinking water • Access to improved sanitation facilities Social insurance and assistance • Access to health insurance • Access to family planning services • Access to conditional cash transfers Awareness, behavior change, and parenting and caring practices • Nutrition and health awareness raising • Provision of interpersonal behavior change counseling • Provision of parenting counseling • Provision of early childhood education, early child stimulation, and child development monitoring • Provision of adolescent reproductive health counseling • Women's empowerment and child protection Food and agriculture • Provision of food assistance for poor and near-poor households • Nutritious food security programs • Access to fortified staple foods • Access to nutritious food product information

Source: World Bank 2020a, 13.
Note: NPER = nutrition public expenditure review.

presents an initial summary list of keywords from 30 countries (Fracassi et al. 2020, annex B). National nutrition strategies and plans are equally important resources that can be helpful to identify relevant keywords. In the process of creating a country-specific list of keywords, it can be useful to review search terms used in other NPERs (box 3.2).[5] Based on a review of these resources, the team should finalize a list of keywords that will be used in the next step. In some instances, the team may need to include variations of the keywords, which could be recorded slightly differently in different parts of the financial management information system/integrated financial management information system (FMIS/IFMIS). For example, to capture expenditures related to iron supplementation, the team may need to specify not just "iron" or "iron supplementation" but also "iron/folic acid supplementation" (because tablets may contain

TABLE 3.2 The *Lancet* framework for programs and interventions, by nutrition category

DEFINING NUTRITION CATEGORIES	PROGRAMS AND INTERVENTIONS
Specific: Direct high-impact nutrition interventions	• Adolescent health and preconception nutrition • Maternal dietary supplementation • Micronutrient supplementation or fortification • Breastfeeding and complementary feeding • Dietary supplementation for children • Dietary diversification • Feeding behaviors and stimulation • Treatment of severe acute malnutrition • Disease prevention and management • Nutrition interventions in emergencies
Sensitive: Indirect nutrition interventions with nutrition-relevant objectives, outcomes, and/or actions	• Agriculture and food security • Social safety nets • Early child development • Maternal mental health • Women's empowerment • Child protection • Classroom education • Water and sanitation • Health and family planning services
Enabling: Interventions that enhance and improve the governance and increase the effectiveness of nutrition interventions	• Rigorous evaluations • Advocacy strategies • Horizontal and vertical coordination • Accountability, incentives regulation, legislation • Leadership programs • Capacity investments • Domestic resource mobilization

Source: Black et al. 2013.
Note: See the *Lancet* framework in appendix A.

both iron and folic acid), "Fe," "(Fe)," "Fe3," "Fe/folic acid," "iron-containing tablets," or other similar terms. Similarly, keywords may need to consider commonly used abbreviation norms (for example, specifying "vitamin A," "vit. A," and "vit A" for vitamin A supplementation).

Step 4. Perform a search of the identified keywords in the electronic government expenditure data set (FMIS/IFMIS) and other data sources (as needed) for each relevant field.[6] A comprehensive classification has the following hierarchical fields: program, subprogram, activity, and output, with each field representing a more disaggregated classification of the former. If further disaggregation is needed, the keyword search can be supplemented with a search in another data set (box 3.3). The search should yield a list of nutrition-relevant budget line items that can be further assessed for inclusion (or not) in the list of nutrition expenditures.

Step 5. Determine whether a nutrition-relevant budget line item (identified in Step 4) satisfies the inclusion criteria to be counted as a nutrition expenditure (determine Yes/No for each budget line item). The NPER team should carefully

BOX 3.2

Examples of keywords used in the Bhutan NPER, by sector/ministry

- *Ministry of Works and Human Settlement:* water, hygiene, sanitation, toilet, sewerage, waste, wash; excluding storm water, irrigation water, bypass road + water, water + hostel
- *Ministry of Environment:* water, hygiene, sanitation, toilet, sewerage, RWSS, waste, wash
- *Ministry of Agriculture and Forests:* livestock + school, vegetable + school
- *Ministry of Health:* water, hygiene, sanitation, toilet, sewerage, waste, wash
- *Gross National Happiness Commission:* food + nutrition, home + garden, vegetable + farming
- *Ministry of Home and Cultural Affairs:* water, hygiene, sanitation, toilet, sewerage, RWSS, waste

Source: World Bank 2019b.
Note: NPER = nutrition public expenditure review.

BOX 3.3

Example from Indonesia of how to perform a keyword search on multiple data sets

In Indonesia, the Ministry of Finance's fiscal data do not include any subclassification beyond broad categories of nutrition spending, which can lead to overestimation of what constitutes nutrition spending. The data contain the categories "sector," "program," and "output," among others. Each program is categorized into outputs, but there is no further subcategory of activities. At the output level, some nutritional interventions are categorized together with non-nutrition interventions. For example, deworming, which is a nutrition intervention, is combined with filariasis—a non-nutrition intervention. Likewise, the output under immunization does not specify the type of vaccination. Instead, the aggregated immunization expenditures include vaccines for pilgrimage and influenza and not just those pertaining to nutrition. To unpack information beyond the output level, the nutrition public expenditure review team needed to analyze activity-level data. For this purpose, the team reviewed the annual work plan and budget data of the Ministry of Health. This data set is an extension of Ministry of Finance data, because it disaggregates output data by subclassification. The team then performed a keyword search on data under the activity field and included only those interventions that were relevant to nutrition.

Source: World Bank 2020a.

craft inclusion criteria to determine whether budget line items identified in Step 4 should be included as part of nutrition financing. The application of this step will likely be straightforward for nutrition-specific budget line items (most will satisfy the criteria and be a Yes in Step 5). However, it is particularly important to apply an inclusion criteria filter to nutrition-sensitive interventions to determine whether they should be included as nutrition expenditures or not. If a budget line item satisfies the inclusion criteria (Yes in Step 5), it should be included as nutrition expenditures in full, without any sort of discounting of costs at this stage. Step 6 will examine whether the budget line item is sufficiently disaggregated. If a budget line items does not satisfy the inclusion criteria (No in Step 5), it should not be counted as nutrition expenditures. Given the lack of evidence on the impact of many nutrition-sensitive interventions, the NPER team should not attempt to use any sort of weights to discount for the impact of nutrition-sensitive interventions, even when such interventions are very costly (box 3.4).[7] This means that Step 5 should be answered in a Yes/No manner for all interventions, including high-cost, nutrition-sensitive interventions such as infrastructure costs. The correct use of weights occurs in Step 7, which involves identifying the share of nutrition in a budget line item that bundles nutrition and non-nutrition activities.

The SUN budget analysis methodology is a good starting point for teams to build their inclusion criteria (MQSUN+ 2020). This methodology includes the following considerations:[8]

- The budget line item clearly reflects a sectoral priority that is included in multisectoral planning efforts for nutrition.
- It is possible to identify the target population in terms of direct and indirect beneficiaries.
  - *Direct beneficiaries.* 1,000-day window of opportunity (pregnant and lactating women and children under two years of age), children, adolescents, and women of reproductive age.
  - *Indirect beneficiaries.* Such as households and communities at risk of malnutrition (segmented by livelihoods, vulnerability, and so on).
- It is possible to define a measurable outcome and recognize where this outcome stands within the nutrition impact pathways (such as in the United Nations' Children's Fund's Conceptual Framework on the Determinants of Maternal and Child Nutrition).

Step 6. Determine whether budget line items (Yes in Step 5) are sufficiently disaggregated between nutrition-related and non-nutrition-related interventions (Yes or No for each budget line item). Ideally, data in the government's FMIS/IFMIS (and other data sources that are used) are sufficiently disaggregated, and the NPER team can easily identify budget lines that correspond to nutrition. In this case, the NPER team should include those budget lines as nutrition expenditures. In most cases, however, there will be at least some line items for which this is not the case. In those instances, the team should proceed to Step 7.

Step 7. For budget line items that are not sufficiently disaggregated (No in Step 6; "bundled operational budget"), determine whether there is sufficient evidence to develop disaggregation weights (Yes or No for each line item that was a No in Step 6). For those budget lines with insufficient disaggregation in budget lines (as is often the case), the most updated guidance from SUN suggests that countries use evidence-based disaggregation weights based on either interviews

BOX 3.4

Guidance on high-cost, nutrition-sensitive budget line items

Even after excluding some line items by using the inclusion criteria described in Step 5, there may be high-cost, nutrition-sensitive interventions that pass the inclusion criteria filter (Yes in Step 5). This could be because the nutrition public expenditure review does not systematically develop or apply inclusion criteria when determining whether a budget line item should be included. Examples of such programs are infrastructure costs (for example, water pipes to provide clean water, school latrines and toilets, village health clinic construction costs, and irrigation programs), broad agriculture support programs for high-nutrient crops (for example, fertilizer subsidies, improved seeds, livestock support, and aquaculture support), cash transfer programs, and school feeding programs. These programs do address underlying causes of malnutrition (and are included in the *Lancet* framework), and many do have improving nutrition as one of their overall program goals. The inclusion of these high-cost line items in the calculation of nutrition expenditures will undoubtedly mean that they will dominate less-costly nutrition-specific line items.

This may seem counterintuitive, and teams may be compelled to use weights as a proxy for the likely contribution of these high-cost, nutrition-sensitive interventions (table B3.4.1). However, using weights as a proxy for an intervention's contribution to nutrition is not consistent with Scaling Up Nutrition guidance, which positions weights as a tool to address the issue of budget line items lacking sufficient disaggregation.

To expand the use of weights as proxy for contribution to nutrition would require solid research findings and evidence on the impact of all nutrition-contributing activities, which are not currently available. In the absence of such evidence, nutrition public expenditure reviews should not use weights to attempt to discount for perceived lower contribution to nutrition of nutrition-sensitive interventions (even when such interventions are very costly). Doing so will likely result in a nutrition-financing landscape in which a very high share (that is, 80–90 percent) of nutrition financing falls under nutrition-sensitive interventions, which is in fact what is reported for most countries.

TABLE B3.4.1 NPER examples of the use of weights as proxies for nutrition contributions

COUNTRY	YEAR	WEIGHTS USED AS PROXIES FOR CONTRIBUTION TO NUTRITION
Bangladesh	2019	No
Bhutan	2020	No
Indonesia	2020	Yes (Assumptions were used on a few large programs based on expert judgment or analysis of administrative data—see annex 1 of the Indonesia NPER for details.)
Nepal	2019	Yes (Each nutrition-sensitive program was provided with weights as a proxy for the proportion of the line item that is contributing to nutritional outcomes—see annex 7 of the Nepal NPER for details.)
Rwanda	2020	No (But weights were used in a sensitivity analysis presented in annex 4-5 of the NPER). Partial attribution was provided to nutrition-sensitive interventions and enabling environment investments. Interventions were classified into quartiles to 100 percent, 75 percent, 50 percent, or 25 percent. Activities that were only marginally relevant were attributed only a 10 percent share.)
Sri Lanka	2020	No
Tanzania	2018	Yes (Based on expert judgment, default value of 10 percent was used when an objective basis could not be determined.)

Sources: Ahmed et al. 2020; Finance Division, Government of the Republic of Bangladesh and UNICEF 2019; Piatti-Fünfkirchen et al. 2020; Tanzania, MoFP and UNICEF 2018; World Bank 2019a, 2020a, 2020b.
Note: The use of weights is not consistent with current Scaling Up Nutrition guidance. NPER = nutrition public expenditure review.

or expert consultation with key stakeholders or document reviews. Doing so could allow the team to accurately establish what proportion of line items can be attributed to nutrition.[9] For example, the Indonesia NPER applied disaggregation weights to the National Health Insurance (Jaminan Kesehatan Nasional) program to determine its contribution to nutrition (box 3.5). If evidence-based disaggregation weights can be constructed (Yes in Step 7), the NPER has the option of applying them to the relevant line items. If that is not the case (No in Step 7), the NPER should use the full cost without the use of more subjective disaggregation weights and noting the possibility of overestimation. In the past, SUN included guidance for NPERs to use less precise normative disaggregation weights.[10] In its updated guidance, however, SUN no longer recommends this practice because of its highly subjective nature.[11] Practitioners need to be fully aware that the use of disaggregation weights is a temporary solution until the accounting system can tag line items at a more detailed level, making the process of weighting redundant.

Personnel cost. Personnel cost is a common form of a bundled budget (No in Step 6). Fracassi et al. (2020) state that in most cases the associated personnel costs are likely to be presented at the ministry level, meaning that it is not possible to know what personnel are allocated to which program or service delivery channel, although in some cases there may be disaggregation at the departmental or program level. The NPER should clearly state how personnel costs are presented in the data source and treated to determine nutrition expenditures. When personnel costs are presented at the ministry level, SUN guidance suggests using the most disaggregated data and estimating the proportion of

---

BOX 3.5

Using weights to assess the contribution of Indonesia's National Health Insurance

Indonesia's Ministry of Health has a single program to provide insurance premium assistance through the National Health Insurance (Jaminan Kesehatan Nasional, JKN) program, with the objective to cover 96.8 million citizens. If the entire JKN budget of 26.7 trillion Indonesian rupiah (Rp; fiscal year 2019) is ascribed as nutrition expenditures, it will be a gross overestimation. Therefore, the Indonesia nutrition public expenditure review used weights according to the following assumptions or steps:

Ministry of Health (024)
- Activity code: 5610. JKN.
- Output code: 501. Number of populations would be covered by JKN.
- Volume: 96.8 million people would be covered by JKN.

- Budget allocation for this activity output: Rp 26.7 trillion (US$1.8 billion).
- Weighting assumptions: Only 2 percent of pregnant women and 10 percent of children under five years old are part of the 96.8 million JKN participants (or weight is 12 percent). It is estimated that only 70 percent of insurance services for pregnant women and children will be related to efforts to reduce stunting.
- Formula: 12 percent × 70 percent × Rp 26.7 trillion.
- Of the total budget of Rp 26.7 trillion, only Rp 2.2 trillion (US$160 million) is assumed to contribute to efforts to reduce stunting (the nutrition goal used in the nutrition public expenditure review).

Source: World Bank, forthcoming.

personnel time dedicated to nutrition-related programs. This means that, to adequately identify personnel allocations, the NPER team needs to (1) decide which of the ministries' core personnel from key sectors are involved in nutrition; and (2) review the functions of these personnel and understand how much time is allocated to identified nutrition-related interventions. If there is not enough information to carry out such an analysis, the default position is to leave out personnel costs reported at the aggregated ministry level and note any potential underestimation.

General principles on using weights. Table 3.3 shows the various ways that existing NPERs have approached the use of disaggregation weights for bundled operational budgets and personnel costs. Given the large variance across NPERs, future NPERs should consider the following general principles when determining whether to use weights:

- Any international comparisons of nutrition spending (total or for subcategories such as nutrition-specific or nutrition-sensitive interventions) must clarify the use of different methodologies across countries.
- Weights should not be used as a proxy to discount for the nutrition impact of nutrition-sensitive interventions, even when such interventions are very costly (see box 3.4).
- When presenting data, indicate whether nutrition-sensitive expenditures are weighted or unweighted. If disaggregation weights are used for bundled budgets (for example, bundled operational budgets, personnel cost), the methodology should be clearly spelled out in an annex.

TABLE 3.3 Use of disaggregation weights for bundled budgets

Weights used or not used

COUNTRY	YEAR	BUNDLED OPERATIONAL BUDGET	PERSONNEL COST
Bangladesh	2019	No	No
Bhutan	2020	No	No
Indonesia	2020	Yes (for example, JKN: 1 percent)[a]	Partly yes (salaries in district-level budgets are included without any weights, but it is unclear whether salaries at the central or village level are included)
Nepal	2019	No	No
Rwanda	2020	No (there are ongoing discussions and reform efforts to make nutrition budget data more granular)	No
Sri Lanka	2020	No	Yes (for each ministry/department that implements nutrition interventions, the ratio of total human resources costs has been estimated with respect to total nonhuman resource costs, and the same ratio of human resource costs has been applied for all nutrition-related expenditures by each ministry)[b]
Tanzania	2018	Yes (The term "apportionment percentage" is used: weights ranged from 0 to 100 percent, based on interview notes and policy documents, and the default value of 10 percent was used if a value could not be determined)	Yes (for ministries, department, agencies, and local government authorities with nutrition-relevant activities, both the budget and expenditures for salaries were included, apportioned by the percentage of nonsalary recurrent and development budget allocations that were deemed to be related to nutrition)

Sources: Ahmed et al. 2020; Finance Division, Government of the Republic of Bangladesh and UNICEF 2019; Piatti-Fünfkirchen et al. 2020; Tanzania, MoFP and UNICEF 2018; World Bank 2019a, 2020a, 2020b.
Note: JKN = Jaminan Kesehatan Nasional (National Health Insurance, Indonesia).
a. See box 3.5 in the main text.
b. However, there were two exceptions: (1) for school programs, teachers' salaries (which represent about 80 percent of total human resource expenditures) were excluded from the assigned human resource costs; and (2) for national water, sanitation, and hygiene programs, human resource costs were not added because these are large-scale programs that are outsourced to firms, and labor costs are largely covered by project costs.

- The NPER should always present unweighted nutrition expenditures (total, nutrition-specific, nutrition-sensitive subtotals) as a reference to allow for comparison with other countries (or future NPERs in that country).

ANALYSIS

Once the country nutrition context is presented, nutrition expenditures are quantified through the steps identified in the previous section, their alignment with the country's nutrition goals is assessed, and the NPER can move on to analysis. Based on the interest, budget, and data availability, the NPER team can decide which types of analyses to carry out. Typical analysis in a sector PER explore (1) expenditure levels and trends, (2) composition, (3) service coverage and use, (4) effectiveness,[12] (5) efficiency, and (6) equity.

Expenditure levels and trends

> Indicative questions that the NPER could address:
> - *What is the most recent year's level of nutrition expenditures?*
> - *How has the level of nutrition expenditures changed over time?*
> - *How does the country's expenditure level compare to relevant comparators?*

To put identified nutrition expenditure data into context, NPERs should present a few key metrics such as expenditure per person or child, share of total government expenditures, and percentage of gross domestic product (GDP; table 3.4). It is recommended that the NPER present such information in multiple standardized ways to enable comparisons over time as well as across countries.[13] For per capita expenditures, it is useful to calculate nutrition-specific and nutrition-sensitive expenditures separately, because there are some benchmark data for nutrition-specific interventions (there are none for nutrition-sensitive interventions).

TABLE 3.4 Selected key metrics in NPERs

COUNTRY	PER CAPITA EXPENDITURES (US$)	% OF TOTAL GOVERNMENT EXPENDITURES	% OF GDP
Bangladesh	18	9	1
Bhutan	29 (nutrition-specific only: 8.15)	3.5	1
Indonesia	8.4	2.6	0.2
Nepal	7	23	0.84
Rwanda	• 5.25 (36 per child under five) • Nutrition-specific only 0.8 (5.8 per child under five)	2.5	n/a
Sri Lanka	39.6	5.2	1
Tanzania	n/a	3.8	0.9

Sources: Ahmed et al. 2020; Finance Division, Government of the Republic of Bangladesh and UNICEF 2019; Piatti-Fünfkirchen et al. 2020; Tanzania, MoFP and UNICEF 2018; World Bank 2019a, 2020a, 2020b.
Note: Methodology used in quantifying nutrition expenditures differs from country to country, so caution should be exercised in comparing these key metrics. NPER = nutrition public expenditure review.

- *Expenditures per person (or per child under the age of five).* On the basis of existing nutrition spending data, Shekar et al. (2017) report that government spending on nutrition is, on average, US$0.85 per child under age five in 15 low-income countries, US$4.66 per child under age five in 13 lower-middle-income countries, and US$8.15 per child under age five in 3 upper-middle-income countries. The same study notes that to reach global nutrition targets would require an additional US$10 per child under age five (beyond current expenditures) for high-impact, nutrition-specific interventions in countries that carry the highest burden of stunting, anemia, and wasting and the lowest rates of breastfeeding.
- *Share of total government expenditures.* In the agriculture sector in Sub-Saharan Africa, the African Union–led Comprehensive Africa Agriculture Development Programme has a target that African countries allocate 10 percent of their total annual budgets toward boosting agricultural productivity. Despite weak compliance, the goal is regularly monitored and reported widely to encourage governments to increase spending on agriculture.[14] Unlike in agriculture, no agreed-on benchmark or tracking systems exist for how much governments should spend on nutrition as a percentage of total expenditures. Countries can, however, look at existing NPERs for relevant comparators.
- *Percentage of GDP.* NPERs can calculate the share of nutrition expenditures in the country's GDP. This value can be referenced against estimates of GDP due to reductions in stunting. Galasso and Wagstaff (2017) estimate that stunting costs 7 percent and 9–10 percent of per capita GDP in Africa and South Asia, respectively; Horton and Steckl (2013) estimate the effect to be about 4–11 percent of per capita GDP in Africa and Asia.

COMPOSITION OF EXPENDITURES

Indicative questions that the NPER could address:

- *What are the main financing sources and their mix?*
- *Who finances what?*
- *What is the broad share of financing for nutrition-specific and nutrition-sensitive interventions?*
- *Which sectors have the highest financing levels for nutrition?*

An important contribution of the NPER is to help the government understand nutrition financing in a multitude of different ways. Most PERs also present the economic composition of expenditures by separating recurrent (that is, wages, salaries, goods, and services) and capital (that is, works and capital goods) expenditures. Such an exercise can provide insights into imbalances in the distribution of expenditures (for example, insufficient funds to cover recurring expenses to maintain existing investments). However, except for vertically administered nutrition interventions for which data on the economic composition of expenditures may be available, most nutrition-related interventions are cross-sectoral or part of larger service delivery systems, which makes it difficult to identify costs related only to nutrition (see the earlier discussion on when weights should and should not be used).

Administrative levels

The NPER needs to examine the breakdown of nutrition expenditures at both the central and subnational government levels by using the institutional framework and funds flow diagram. Insights into the distribution of spending by level of government can clarify spending responsibilities. Identifying the administrative level where expenditures are made can help the NPER team identify where accountability lies for challenges related to the execution of spending and help determine how disaggregated the analysis needs to be. For example, the Bhutan NPER found that nutrition expenditures are more decentralized than spending in other sectors. Unlike the 70:30 breakdown of total government expenditures between central and subnational authorities, nutrition-related expenditures were split more evenly between the central and subnational levels.

Nutrition categories

The NPER also needs to examine the breakdown of spending between the broad nutrition categories agreed to in Step 2. These categories include nutrition-specific/nutrition-sensitive interventions and the enabling environment.[15] In all NPERs, nutrition-sensitive spending represents the largest share of spending on nutrition because it spans multiple sectors and a variety of projects, including interventions not directly targeted at nutrition (but addressing underlying conditions that affect nutrition; table 3.5). As stated in earlier in the section on identifying nutrition expenditures, examples include high-cost, nutrition-sensitive interventions such as the construction of pipes for potable water or irrigation canals and fertilizer distribution programs to support crop diversification.

No international benchmark percentage exists that indicates an optimal split between nutrition-specific and nutrition-sensitive interventions. Rather, it depends on the specific country context. Also, an international comparison can be misleading, given the different methodologies countries use to report on

TABLE 3.5 Breakdown of expenditures by broad nutrition categories

COUNTRY	NUTRITION-SPECIFIC (%): NUTRITION-SENSITIVE (%)
Bangladesh	2:98
Bhutan	30:70
Indonesia	10:90
Nepal	13:87
Rwanda[a]	16:80
Sri Lanka	10:90
Tanzania[b]	2:96

Sources: Ahmed et al. 2020; Finance Division, Government of the Republic of Bangladesh and UNICEF 2019; Piatti-Fünfkirchen et al. 2020; Tanzania, MoFP and UNICEF 2018; World Bank 2019a, 2020a, 2020b.
Note: The methodology used in quantifying nutrition expenditures differs from country to country, so these key metrics should be viewed with some caution.
a. In addition, 4 percent for enabling environment.
b. In addition, 2 percent for "unknown/multiple" when the budget line was deemed to include both nutrition-specific and nutrition-sensitive interventions but no one category was thought to dominate. In practice, this category was reserved for nutrition-related local government salaries and medical supplies.

FIGURE 3.6
Breakdown of nutrition-specific and nutrition-sensitive spending

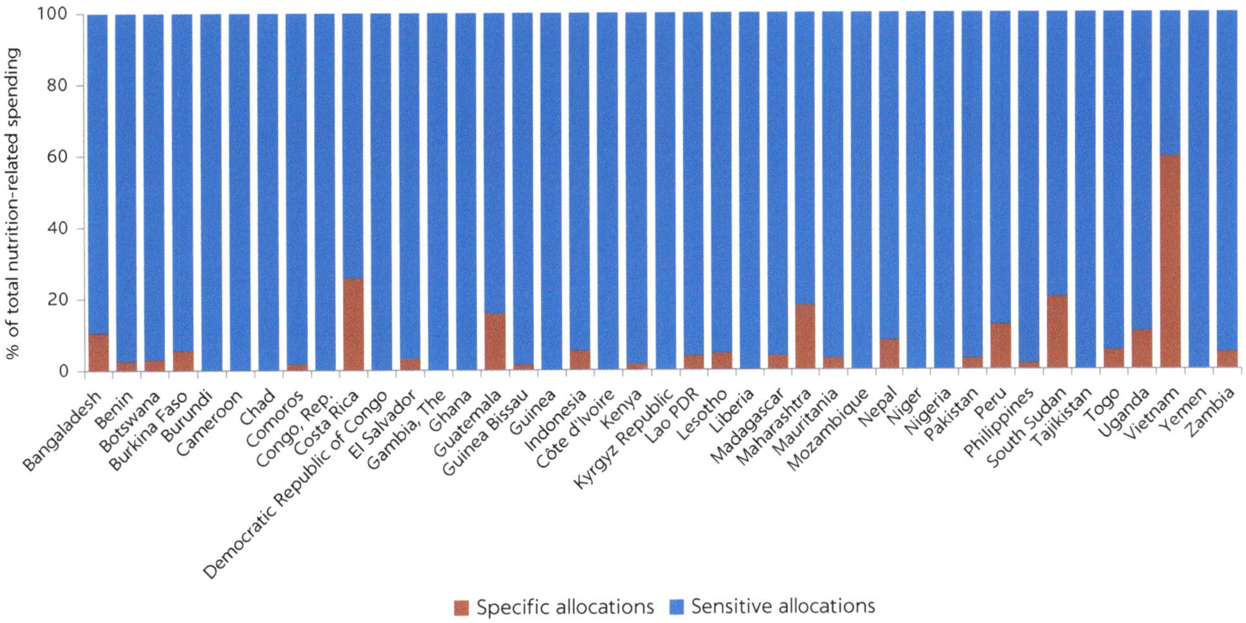

Source: Development Initiatives 2017.

nutrition financing. As an illustrative example, figure 3.6 presents nutrition spending (budget allocation, not actual spending) as reported by countries to SUN and presented in the 2017 *Global Nutrition Report* (Development Initiatives 2017). The share of nutrition-specific spending in most countries is less than 10 percent, with Vietnam being a major outlier because its nutrition-specific spending is higher than nutrition-sensitive spending.

Sector composition

NPERs need to examine the sector composition of public expenditures and identify major programs that have been identified as nutrition expenditures. This is often done separately for nutrition-specific and nutrition-sensitive interventions. In the Sri Lanka NPER, the team identified three program areas that contributed about 90 percent of all nutrition-sensitive investments: (1) the Samurdhi (cash-assistance) welfare program (39 percent); (2) agricultural food security programs, particularly fertilizer subsidies (29 percent); and (3) water sanitation and hygiene programs (25 percent). Two interventions alone represented 80 percent of all nutrition-specific interventions: the fortified food supplement program (Thriposha) and the school meal program.

Service coverage and use

Indicative questions that NPERs could address:

- *What are the coverage and use of proven high-impact nutrition interventions across sectors?*

- *What is the distribution pattern of services across geographical areas and socioeconomic factors?*

> - *What are some bottlenecks to implementing effective interventions?*
> - *What are the key critical intervention gaps?*

It may be useful to present some trends of key nutrition metrics based on the theory of change of the country's nutrition strategy. Data on the service coverage and use of selected key cross-sectoral interventions would serve as key links between system inputs and outcomes, and provide interim evidence of how countries are performing in terms of achieving their nutrition goals. This evidence would provide the basis for a subsequent analysis to be performed in the NPERs (that is, efficiency, effectiveness, and equity) that, among others, assesses the link between financing and outcomes. In the absence of a standard minimum set of interventions and its performance measurement indicators, a results framework (or log frame) associated with national nutrition strategies could help NPER teams identify a set of relevant interventions and indicators for analysis. Global benchmark and reference lists of essential nutrition services, such as the *Lancet* framework and the World Health Organization's Essential Nutrition Actions, could also be consulted. The analysis, whenever possible, should investigate service use at all levels, focusing on its distribution across government administrative levels, socioeconomic quintiles, gender, and the urban/rural split, as well as between different levels of service delivery platforms (for example, curative care from higher-level health facilities, preventive and promotive services at primary health care facilities, and community outreach).

It is essential that the NPER includes a robust theory of change or pathways of impact that demonstrate how interventions contribute to the achievement of nutrition outcomes. Table 3.6 presents how a results framework can be constructed for nutrition-specific and nutrition-sensitive outcomes using the results framework presented in Nepal's Multi-Sector Nutrition Plan: 2018–2022 (National Planning Commission 2017). Nepal's results indicators consist of four levels developed through a thorough theory of change analysis: (1) "Goal (Impact)," which primarily reflects the six World Health Assembly global nutrition targets; (2) "Outcomes" grouped into nutrition-specific and nutrition-sensitive interventions and the enabling environment; (3) "Outputs" with service use level indicators; and (4) "Key Activities," which can also serve as indicators because they have specified annual targets. Although the terminology to define the levels varies by country, it is important that the framework is based on a theory of change and has a concrete set of service use and activity level indicators that support each of the higher-level outcomes and goals. Nepal's Multi-Sector Nutrition Plan: 2018–2022 also sets a target value for each of these indicators for each year of implementation, which can be referred to when assessing the effectiveness of the investment made (appendix B).

Effectiveness

> Indicative questions that the NPER could address:
> - *Are programs delivering the intended nutrition outputs and outcomes?*
> - *Is there any correlation between expenditures for certain programs and nutrition output and outcome indicators that those programs target?*

TABLE 3.6 Results framework of Nepal's Multi-Sector Nutrition Plan: 2018–2022

GOAL (IMPACT): IMPROVED MATERNAL, ADOLESCENT, AND CHILD NUTRITION BY SCALING UP ESSENTIAL NUTRITION-SPECIFIC AND NUTRITION-SENSITIVE INTERVENTIONS AND CREATING AN ENABLING ENVIRONMENT FOR NUTRITION	BASELINE	TARGETS				
		2018	2019	2020	2021	2022
• Prevalence of stunting among children under 5 years reduced						
• Prevalence of wasting among children under 5 years reduced						
• Prevalence of low birth weight reduced						
• % reduction in children under 5 years with overweight and obesity						
• % reduction in overweight and obese WRA						
• % of women with chronic energy deficiency (measured as body mass index) reduced						
Outcome 1 (Nutrition-Specific): Improved access to and equitable use of nutrition-specific services						
• Increased % of children aged 6–23 months having minimum acceptable diet						
• Reduced % of anemia among children aged 6–59 months						
• Reduced % of anemia among adolescent girls (10–19 years)						
• Reduced % of anemia among WRA (15–49 years)						
• Reduced prevalence of children under 5 years with diarrhea in last two weeks						
Outcome 2 (Nutrition-Sensitive): Improved access to and equitable use of nutrition-sensitive services and improved healthy habits and practices						
• Reduced proportion of population below minimum level of dietary energy consumption						
• Increased % people using safe drinking water						
• Increased % people using improved sanitation facilities that are not shared						
• Increased % of people practicing hand washing with soap and water before feeding baby (0–2 years) and after cleaning babies' bottoms						
• Percentage of women aged 20–24 years who are married or in union before age 18						
• Increased gross enrollment rate (boys and girls) in early child education and development/preprimary education						
• Decreased % of out-of-school children (boys and girls) in basic education						
• Increased basic education cycle completion rate (boys and girls)						
Outcome 3 (Enabling Environment): Improved policies, plans, and multisectoral coordination at the federal, provincial, and local government levels to enhance the nutrition status of all population groups						
• Percentage of farmland owned by women or in joint ownership						
• Number of local, provincial, and federal government plans that include nutrition and food security programs in line with MSNP-II						
• Availability of national MSNP-II document						
• Availability of national budget code for nutrition and food security						
• National Capacity Development Master Plan for implementation of MSNP-II produced						
• Multisector commitment and resources for nutrition increase to at least 3.5% of total government budget						
• Financial resource tracking in place						

Source: Adapted from National Planning Commission 2017, annex 1.
Note: MSNP-II = Multi-Sector Nutrition Plan: 2018–2022; WRA = women of reproductive age.

The ultimate objective of nutrition financing is to achieve intended nutrition outcomes. The NPER investigates the broader question of whether nutrition investments address the objectives presented in the country's nutrition strategy. An assessment of the effectiveness of public expenditures focuses on whether spending delivers the outcomes targeted by the government's strategic plans.[16]

Bhutta et al. (2013), in the 2013 *Lancet* series on maternal and child nutrition, identify a list of interventions that have been assessed to reduce child deaths resulting from malnutrition. However, the effectiveness of each intervention depends on the specific local context and how the intervention is delivered, such as the level and local determinants of malnutrition, differences in the characteristics of beneficiaries (including age), the availability of service infrastructure, and the government's implementation capacity. A review of impact evaluations by the World Bank shows that interventions that are found to be effective in a randomized controlled trial in a research setting often deliver different results when implemented under field conditions in different settings (Independent Evaluation Group 2010).

Properly assessing effectiveness requires impact evaluations of major nutrition programs, which are typically outside the scope of an NPER. However, the NPER team should review the literature for recent impact evaluations of major programs (as identified in the NPER) and use the main findings to formulate reform options or recommendations. Alternatively, the NPER itself could be used as an entry point to carry out future impact evaluations of major programs.

In the absence of impact evaluations, the effectiveness of nutrition spending can be explored by comparing trends in expenditures and outcomes. Box 3.6 gives an example from Mozambique's health-focused PER, which constructed a graph that compares trends in expenditures and outcomes, followed by a qualitative analysis to understand what drives the identified trends on how to evaluate the effectiveness of public spending (World Bank 2016b).

Efficiency

Indicative questions that the NPER could address:

- *[Allocative efficiency] Can the distribution of spending be improved to increase the output?*

- *[Technical efficiency] Are major nutrition programs executed in a cost-effective manner?*

- *[Administrative efficiency] What is the status of spending relative to plans and commitments? How much of the budget has been executed?*

One of the important objectives of a PER is to examine how efficiently public resources are used a country. The most common types of efficiency examined are the following:

- *Allocative efficiency,* which measures the extent to which resources are distributed to the most appropriate interventions to maximize impact. It examines whether and how much resources should be allocated to one activity or program instead of another to achieve the least costly intervention mix that will yield the highest impact.
- *Technical efficiency*,[17] which measures the extent to which resources are spent efficiently (within an intervention) given allocated funds and assesses whether an intervention yields a given set of outputs at least cost.

BOX 3.6

Assessing the effectiveness of health spending in Mozambique

An effectiveness analysis of health spending requires a comparison of trends in health financing and outcomes, and an analysis of factors driving the trends.

Comparison of trends. Figure B3.6.1 shows health spending per capita in Mozambique against key intermediate outcomes: the combined diphtheria, tetanus, and pertussis vaccine; the measles-containing vaccine dose 1; and the percentage of assisted deliveries, all of which ultimately contribute to reducing child mortality (one of the country's long-term objectives). Despite some fluctuations, per capita health financing has been increasing steadily, especially since 2010. Health outcomes, however, show a relatively flatter trend over the same period, which raises questions about the effectiveness of health spending in Mozambique.

Analysis of factors driving the trends. An analysis of the factors driving health expenditures and outcomes in Mozambique revealed that the rise in per capita health expenditures, especially since 2010, was due to an increase in health financing under the vertical fund component (off-budget donor financing), which was fueled by the United States' President's Emergency Plan for AIDS Relief. The relative flattening of vaccination and assisted delivery trends in this period, despite a rise in per capita health spending, is not surprising because most of the rise in spending was earmarked for HIV/AIDS. In fact, there was a marked improvement in antiretroviral coverage between 2011 and 2013, from 49 percent to 84 percent among pregnant women, and from 18 percent to 32 percent among the general population. More balanced spending would serve to improve other key indicators, thereby increasing the overall effectiveness of health spending.

FIGURE B3.6.1
Health spending per capita in Mozambique, by key outcome, 1995–2013

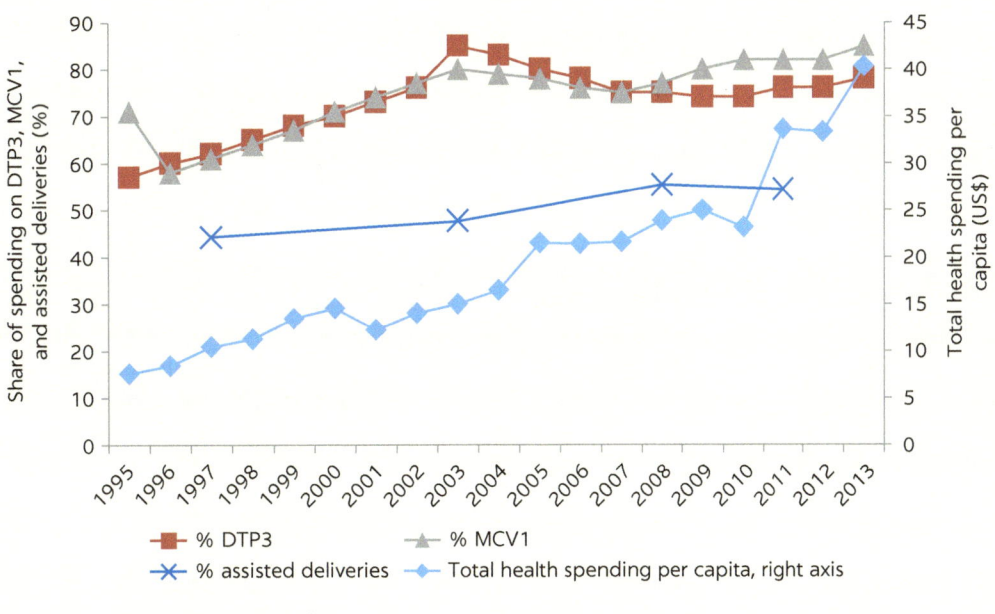

Source: World Bank 2016b.
Note: DTP3 = diphtheria, tetanus, and pertussis vaccine; MCV1 = measles-containing vaccine dose 1.

Source: World Bank 2016b.

- *Administrative efficiency,* which measures the difference between budget allocations and actual expenditures; this information can provide insights into areas in need of process improvements to improve performance and, ultimately, final outcomes.

Allocative efficiency

An allocative efficiency analysis often starts with a description of the distribution of expenditures across interventions, activities, and programs. It examines whether expenditures are directed to proven cost-effective interventions and provides insights into the efficiency of nutrition expenditures. For example, global evidence suggests that antenatal micronutrient supplementation, balanced energy-protein supplementation during pregnancy, vitamin A supplementation for children, and the promotion of infant and young child feeding (IYCF) practices are some of the most cost-effective interventions to reduce under-five stunting (Shekar et al. 2017). Therefore, it will be important for the NPER to assess the types of expenditures and the coverage of interventions and suggest whether there is room for improvement in resource allocation, considering the country's specific nutrition situation.

Several exercises (including NPERs and other nutrition-related case studies) highlight potential inefficiencies in nutrition services by identifying the least cost-effective interventions. For example, the Sri Lanka NPER identified the high cost of its fortified food supplementation program, Thriposha, and revealed it was ineffective in addressing acute undernutrition. It proposed a shift in strategy to targeted measures that ensure supplements are used only by those in need. Moreover, the Bhutan NPER found that the country's largest nutrition expenditures were related to the national school feeding program, which does not directly address childhood stunting among children under the age of five.

Optima Nutrition, a resource optimization tool, can provide policy makers with important guidance for targeting nutrition investments to maximize their impact.[18] This quantitative tool can be used as part of a wider NPER exercise to estimate how to target resources to improve nutrition outcomes and overall allocative efficiency. Optima Nutrition focuses on the current expenditure distribution and intervention coverage and analyzes the marginal benefits of allocating funds to a mix of interventions or geographical areas. It then suggests optimized allocation scenarios (either within the same financing envelope or a given amount of additional funding) that can maximize outcomes.

Several countries have used Optima Nutrition to prioritize nutrition-related interventions and allocate budgets across nutrition programs. For example, it was used in the Bangladesh NPER to simulate an optimal mix of interventions to minimize child mortality and stunting. The study found that investments in priority interventions, such as the promotion of improved IYCF and vitamin A supplementation in Dhaka and Chittagong—regions with the greatest number of stunted children—could increase the cumulative number of children without stunting by 1.3 million (5 percent). This outcome could be achieved without any extra resources (US$0.75 per person in need per year). The Rwanda NPER also used the Optima Nutrition tool to evaluate alternative strategies for allocating spending to improve outcomes. Three scenarios were tested to identify how nutrition outcomes would vary depending on a choice of high-impact interventions.[19] The analysis found that scenario 3 was the optimal because it achieves the best outcomes on all indicators except for the stunting effect in scenario 1, which optimized only on stunting figures but not any of the other nutrition outcomes (figure 3.7).

FIGURE 3.7
Example from the Rwanda NPER: Optima simulation result

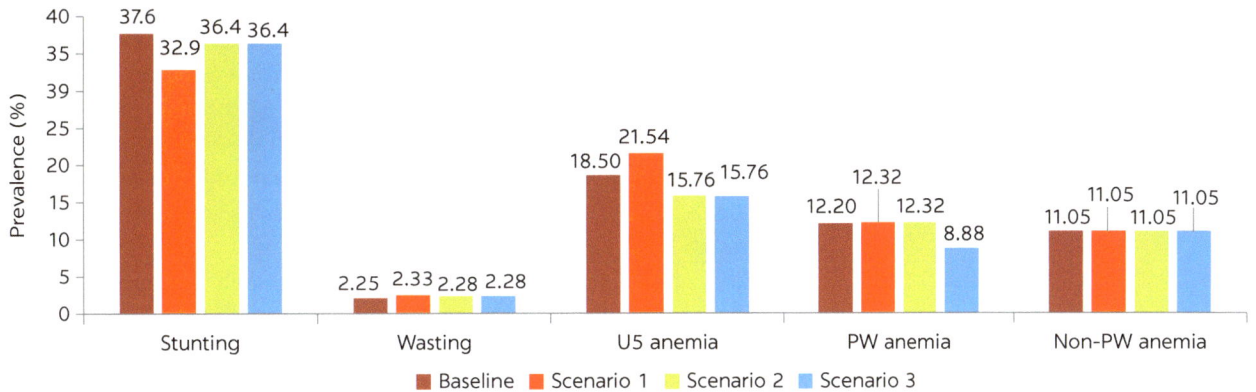

Source: World Bank 2020b.
Note: Scenario 1: Increasing the number of alive, nonstunted children; Scenario 2: Increasing the number of alive, nonstunted, and nonanemic children; and Scenario 3: Increasing the number of alive, nonstunted children, and nonanemic children, and minimizing anemia and mortality among pregnant women. PW = pregnant women; U5 = under 5 years old.

Using high-quality data collected through an NPER in the Optima Nutrition analysis can provide vital information to influence spending decisions. While the Optima Nutrition analysis can inform improved resource allocation for nutrition interventions through a modeling approach, it can also influence a country's budgetary process if it builds on costing data generated through a robust analysis of actual budgets. If the NPER is designed to generate or identify granular expenditure data for high-impact nutrition interventions that can be incorporated into the Optima Nutrition analysis, insights from both analyses using the same costing data could be used to identify gaps and determine an optimal allocation of public resources.

Technical efficiency

Nutrition interventions are often bundled with other health and non-health-related interventions. Even within the health sector, malnutrition, for example, is addressed in conjunction with interventions aimed at improving maternal and child health more broadly (for example, nutrition messaging and supplementation provided during antenatal care visits). For this reason, none of the existing NPERs to date have carried out a technical efficiency analysis, and thus this subsection presents relevant examples from health sector PERs.[20]

Technical efficiency measures the appropriateness of the level of inputs used within a given intervention.[21] An intervention is technically inefficient if the same (or greater) outcome can be produced with less of one type of input (Shiell et al. 2002). Some leading sources of technical inefficiency related to health system inputs include an inappropriate or costly staff mix; underuse and overpricing of generic drugs; overuse of procedures, investigations, and equipment; inappropriate hospital admissions or length of stay; number of patients seen by a doctor or health provider; and inappropriate size of hospital. Understanding the causes of inefficiencies can help countries correct operational inefficiencies. For example, the Ethiopian health sector PER showed that the country's health facilities were operating at low efficiency, with one health worker seeing two to nine outpatients and just one inpatient per day (World Bank 2016a). Moreover, the review found that low productivity of health workers was associated with a host of factors, including a lack of equipment at health facilities.

The nonparametric data envelopment analysis (DEA) is a tool that can also be used to measure technical efficiency. The DEA produces an efficiency score ranging from 0 percent (inefficient) to 100 percent (efficient). For instance, a Zambian study using a DEA found that Zambian hospitals were operating at a 67 percent level of efficiency, which meant that significant resources were being wasted. The study found that merging or downgrading hospitals could help to improve the overall efficiency of the country's hospitals (Masiye 2007). In the health sector, some commonly used indicators, such as number of consultations per physician or hospital bed occupancy rate, are often used to measure technical efficiency. In agriculture, crop yield, or the amount of crop that can be harvested from a plot of land (tons per hectare), is a commonly measured metric of technical efficiency. Such indicators have not yet been established for nutrition. Also, even for situations when data are available, detailed data on program implementation are typically required (for example, a DEA on antenatal care requires data on inputs [staff, capital, recurring expenses] and outputs [number of antenatal consultations offered]), which may require survey work at primary care facilities, in addition to health facility records, making this a data-intensive exercise.

Administrative efficiency

Administrative efficiency measures deviations in the budget process between financial commitments and their execution (at either the sector or the program level), which reflects the quality of budgetary planning as well as implementation efficiency. It is often measured in terms of the budget execution rate, which is the ratio of actual expenditures to the allocated budget. If development partner (DP) financing accounts for a significant share of nutrition financing, the NPER would ideally present the absorption rate of both the government budget and the off-budget DP financing. For the government budget, the execution rate is often used to measure the deviation of spending from the budget; for DP financing, the disbursement rate measures the deviation of actual disbursement from commitment. Given the multisectoral nature of nutrition financing, execution rates should be examined across ministries and between different levels of government, depending on data availability. Equipped with an understanding of the differences between budget allocations and actual expenditures, policy makers are in a better position to revise spending commitments and improve administrative capacity during the next planning cycle.

For example, the Bhutan NPER includes a comparison of budget execution rates between different levels of government and across ministries. It reveals that the budget execution capacity of the Ministry of Health is 30 percentage points higher than that of the Ministry of Works and Human Settlements (figure 3.8). Failure to spend available funds may be due to limited capacity at the spending agency or delayed or insufficient budget release (from the Ministry of Finance to the line ministry, or from the ministry to local agencies) that prevents the implementation of planned expenditures. The NPER analyzed the differences in execution rates and found that the relatively low absorptive capacity of the Ministry of Works and Human Settlements resulted from procurement delays for large infrastructure investments, highlighting a major area of administrative inefficiency.

Budget execution rates can also be estimated for different interventions to reveal administrative inefficiencies related to specific programs. The Indonesia NPER shows varying execution rates across different interventions, ranging

FIGURE 3.8
Example from the Bhutan NPER: Absorption rates for nutrition-related interventions by ministry

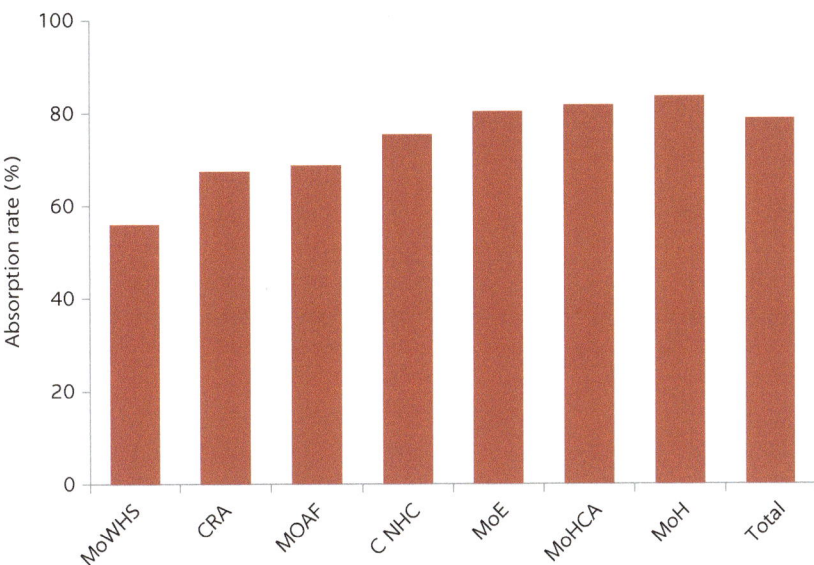

Source: Ahmed et al. 2020.
Note: CRA = Council for Religious Affairs; GNHC = Gross National Happiness Commission; MoAF = Ministry of Agriculture and Forests; MoE = Ministry of Education; MoH = Ministry of Health; MoHCA = Ministry of Home and Cultural Affairs; MoWHS = Ministry of Works and Human Settlement.

FIGURE 3.9
Example from the Indonesia NPER: Budget execution by intervention

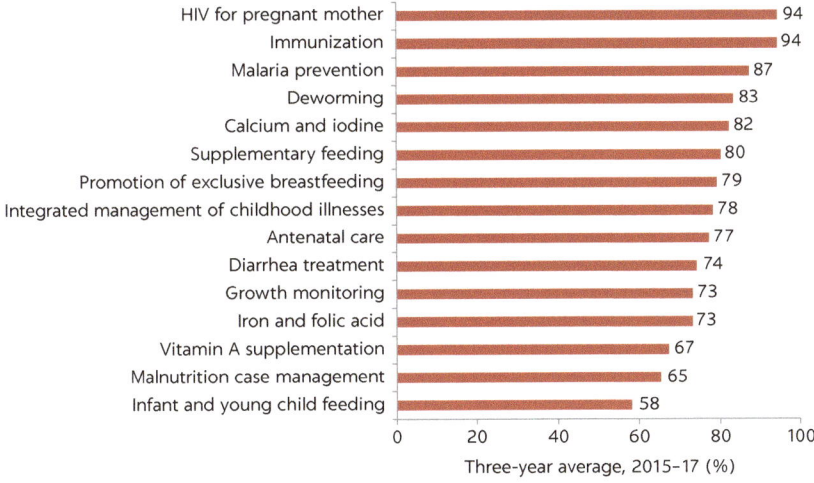

Source: World Bank 2020a.
Note: NPER = nutrition public expenditure review.

from immunization programs, which had the highest execution rates, to IYCF programs, which had the lowest execution rates (figure 3.9). It also shows that actual public expenditures in Indonesia are, on average, 22 percentage points lower than planned expenditures. In addition to the absorption rate analysis, the team performed a qualitative analysis to explain the differences in absorption rates (box 3.7).

> **BOX 3.7**
>
> ### Potential bottlenecks in the flow of funds in Indonesia
>
> In Indonesia, more than five ministries and 20 laws govern the management and operation of village-level institutions, which are responsible for stunting-related interventions. At the central level, ministries provide policy, regulatory, and infrastructure investment support as well as guidance related to capacity building and technical assistance. Fiscal transfers flow from the central to the district level, the latter of which is responsible for funding operational activities such as health service delivery and water supply and sewage management. Before 2014, districts were responsible for supporting village-level activities; however, districts did not always carry out the transfers to the village level, which resulted in bottlenecks in accessing funding. To resolve these bottlenecks, the national government implemented two new direct transfers from the central to the village level. Despite the two new direct transfers, the nutrition public expenditure review identified additional bottlenecks in the flow of funds that were due to the proliferation of channels through which money was transferred. These multiple ways to transfer funds made it difficult to track the transfers and evaluate potential inefficiencies in the disbursement of funds.
>
> In addition, the national health insurance agency reimburses providers such as village midwives directly for their services. Midwives who fall under district health centers that have financial autonomy receive payments through these health centers and not directly from the national health insurance agency. Most district health centers do not, however, have financial autonomy and do not receive direct transfers from the national health insurance agency. Instead, they pay the midwives through transfers made to district health offices, which transfer the funds to district health centers. These payment mechanisms vary across districts. Because of this convoluted payment structure, many village midwives do not receive their payments.
>
> *Source:* World Bank 2020a.

Most low- and middle-income countries rely on external financing to implement their public programs. In these countries, the execution of planned interventions depends in some cases on the timely disbursement of financing from DPs. Depending on the availability of data on committed and disbursed funds from DPs, the NPER could also present information on actual disbursement. Understanding the actual disbursement rate can inform the design and implementation of corrective policies.

The Ethiopia health sector PER examined trends in committed and disbursed DP funds managed by the Federal Ministry of Health over a period of five years. To harmonize on-budget financial assistance from DPs, policy makers in Ethiopia implemented a range of measures, including the establishment of the Grant Management Unit within the Federal Ministry of Health in 2008–09. As a result, committed and disbursed funds from DPs have converged over time, reflecting an improvement in the disbursement rate from 55 percent in 2008–09 to 96 percent in 2012–13 (figure 3.10).

The Rwanda NPER used self-reported data from the country's key DPs to examine trends in off-budget financing. It found significant complementarity between government and DP funding for nutrition activities. For example, DPs focused on sectors such as agriculture and food security and areas such as micronutrient supplementation; the government focused on water and sanitation as well as malaria interventions. For nutrition-enhancing activities, DPs focused mainly on capacity building, whereas the government focused on accountability incentives, regulation, and legislation (box 3.8).

FIGURE 3.10
Example from the Ethiopia health sector PER: External assistance managed by the Ministry of Health

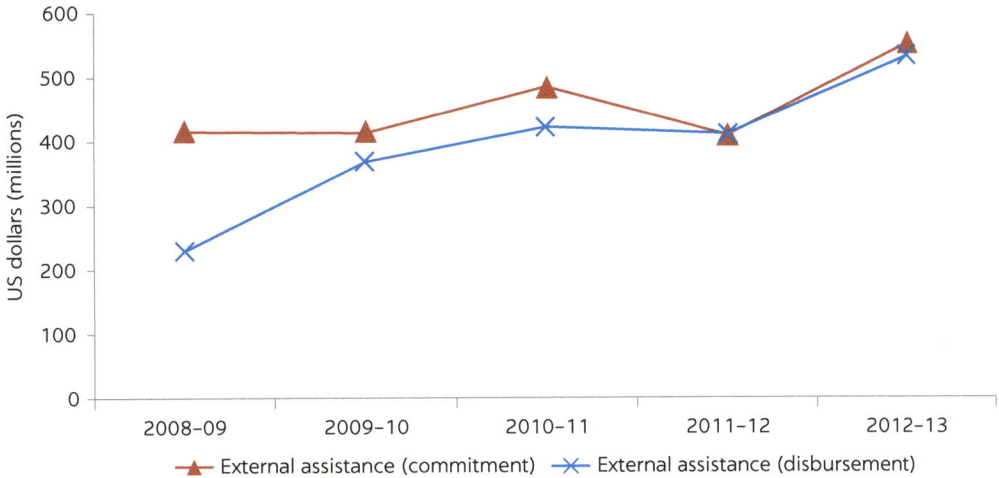

Source: World Bank 2016a.
Note: PER = public expenditure review.

BOX 3.8

Collecting data on off-budget external nutrition financing in Rwanda

Rwanda first conducted a mapping of its development partners working on nutrition in its Joint Action Plan to Eliminate Malnutrition 2016–2020. To gather more data on off-budget nutrition spending, the nutrition public expenditure review team requested that all 23 key development partners in the country fill out a spreadsheet with self-reported information on their nutrition-related expenditure. They needed to specify the time period and categorize nutrition-related spending into nutrition-specific, nutrition-sensitive, and nutrition-enabling interventions. Information received from the development partners was later cross-checked to ensure accuracy and consistency.

Source: World Bank 2020b.

Equity

Indicative questions that the NPER could address:

- *Have expenditures focused on areas most in need?*
- *Has spending benefited the most vulnerable?*
- *Does spending target geographical areas or subpopulations that lag in certain outcomes?*

An equity analysis of nutrition spending assumes that populations and geographical areas with higher levels of malnutrition should have a correspondingly higher level of spending. This type of analysis needs access to data on (1) the most deprived groups or areas (that is, groups or areas where the burden of malnutrition is the greatest); and (2) the nature and scale of investments directed to different groups or geographical regions. For example, Bhutan's nutrition spending is considered fairly equitable, because the Eastern region, which has the highest stunting rate, also has highest level of per capita nutrition-related spending (table 3.7).[22]

Graphical representation of subnational expenditures and nutrition outcomes is illustrative to highlight geographical equity. The Tanzania NPER presents a plot of district-level nutrition spending per child under the age of five against the stunting rate for 22 representative sample districts (figure 3.11). The figure shows that spending appears to increase broadly with stunting levels;

TABLE 3.7 Example from the Bhutan NPER: Subnational nutrition-related expenditures, 2016–17

REGION	PER CAPITA NUTRITION-RELATED EXPENDITURES (NU)	STUNTING RATE
Western	1,124	16.2
Central	1,793	18.5
Eastern	2,118	29.1

Source: World Bank 2019b.
Note: NPER = nutrition public expenditure review; Nu = Bhutanese ngultrum (Nu 1.00 = approximately US$0.014).

FIGURE 3.11

Example from the Tanzania NPER: District-level nutrition spending per child under five plotted against the stunting rate

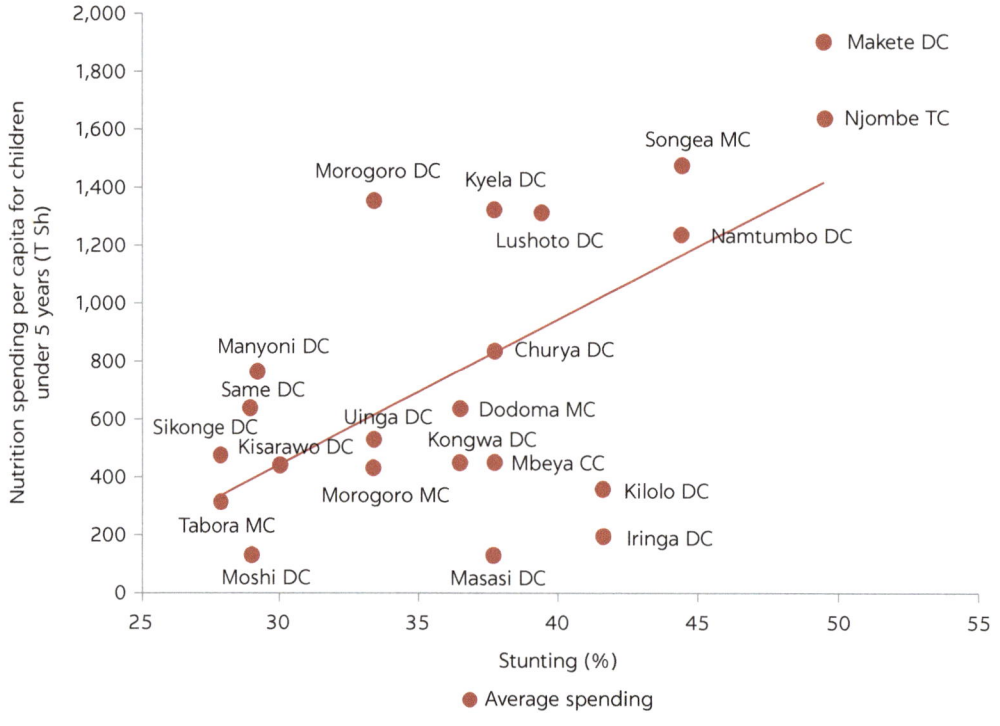

Source: Tanzania, MoFP and UNICEF 2018.
Note: CC = city council; DC = district council; MC = municipal council; NPER = nutrition public expenditure review; TC = town council; T Sh = Tanzania shilling.

however, the NPER notes that most values are clustered in the lower half of the graph regardless of the stunting level, and that a full benefit incidence analysis (BIA) is necessary to draw any conclusions.

Ideally, a BIA can be performed as part of the PER to reveal inequity in the allocation and use of health resources.[23] The BIA combines the cost of providing public services with information on their use to generate distributions of the benefit of government spending. It is used to provide insights into what extent governments spend on services that improve the lives of the poor. The basic premise of a BIA is that the poor are disadvantaged in gaining access to important basic services (for example, nutrition) that would help them escape poverty. It suggests an active role for the government to provide these services to poor and vulnerable groups (Demery 2000).

A BIA requires data on government spending on a service, public use of the service, and the socioeconomic characteristics of the population using the service. Government spending data are typically obtained either from the ministry of finance (FMIS/IFMIS) or the relevant line ministry. It can be challenging to access disaggregated spending data by administrative level because not all countries have comprehensive spending data on nutrition services. The second and third types of data—the use of the service, and socioeconomic characteristics of the population using the service—can be obtained from household surveys. For instance, a BIA of health services could use surveys such as Demographic and Health Surveys and Living Standards Surveys that include health-related indicators, although there are some data limitations to compute service use rates and rank service users by socioeconomic quintile.[24]

The BIA is applied in the health sector largely to assess the appropriateness of the distribution of benefits from using health services relative to the need for care. The BIA can be presented in several different ways, including through a concentration index or a dominance test.[25] For example, as part of the Zambia health sector PER, a BIA was commissioned to assess the distributional impact of health reforms on public spending and equity using the Zambia Household Expenditure and Utilization Survey. The BIA results show that the distribution of benefits for both inpatient and outpatient services at all public health facilities

TABLE 3.8 **Example from the Zambia health sector PER: BIA results on the distribution of outpatient and inpatient services**

PROVIDER/FACILITY TYPE	OUTPATIENT			INPATIENT		
	CI	SE	DT	CI	SE	DT
Public						
Tertiary (3rd-level) hospitals	0.523***	0.065	–	0.528***	0.044	–
General (2nd-level) hospitals	0.385***	0.032	–	0.222***	0.033	–
District (1st-level) hospitals	0.091**	0.037	–	−0.090*	0.052	+
Health centers	0.013	0.018	n-Dom	−0.179***	0.022	+
All hospitals (3rd+2nd+1st)	0.214***	0.024	–	0.243***	0.015	–
All health facilities (hospitals and health centers)	0.046**	0.018	–	0.160***	0.017	–
All health facilities (inpatient and outpatient)	0.059***	0.018	–			
Mission health facilities	−0.106	0.068	+	−0.158*	0.091	+
Private health facilities	0.686***	0.027	–	0.804***	0.071	–

Source: World Bank 2019b.
Note: BIA = benefit incidence analysis; CI = concentration index; DT = dominance test; n-Dom = nondominance; PER = public expenditure review; SE = standard error; – means that the 45-degree line dominates (pro-rich); + means that the concentration curve dominates (pro-poor).
*$p < 0.1$ **$p < 0.05$ ***$p < 0.01$.

(all types of hospitals and health centers) and private health facilities is generally pro-rich (table 3.8). However, the distribution of inpatient services for public district hospitals, public health centers, and mission health facilities is pro-poor.

NOTES

1. This information is available at the Institute for Health Metrics and Evaluation's website (http://www.healthdata.org/gbd/gbd-2019-resources).
2. These six indicators are the indicators tracked under the global nutrition targets endorsed by the World Health Assembly in 2012, which were subsequently adopted as Sustainable Development Goal 2 nutrition targets. See the World Health Organization's Global database on the Implementation of Nutrition Action (GINA) policy web page (https://extranet.who.int/nutrition/gina/en/node/11519#:~:text=By%20the%20year%202020%2C%20the,and%20obesity%2Foverweight%20will%20be) and Global Targets 2025 web page (https://www.who.int/teams/nutrition-and-food-safety/global-targets-2025).
3. None of the NPERs to date has addressed overweight and obesity when examining the performance of nutrition expenditures.
4. If the NPER has a significant emphasis on these institutional issues, the team may consider calling the document a nutrition public expenditure and institutional review. Thus far, only one such document exists: the Rwanda nutrition public expenditure and institutional review (Piatti-Fünfkirchen et al. 2020).
5. The Indonesia NPER used a list of keywords to include as well as a list of keywords to exclude. This option may be helpful if local experts can determine common inclusion errors from past work. For example, for food supplementation programs, some keywords to include are "food supplementation," "provision of milk for children under 5," and "*taburia* (multiple micronutrient supplements for children)"; some keywords to exclude are "*lansia* (elderly people)," "patient," and "whitening" (Indonesia Ministry of National Development Planning, National Development Planning Agency, and Indonesia Ministry of Finance 2018).
6. Data sources on nutrition financing presented in the chapter 2 subsection titled "Data sources for nutrition financing" should be used in this step.
7. ACF International, Save the Children, and SUN Senegal (2017) present an alternative methodology that was used in the nutrition budget analysis by Burkina Faso in 2016. This alternative methodology makes a lot of sense but has high data requirements and is not discussed in the SUN guidance. The methodology introduces two separate weights (W1 = portion of budget allocated to nutrition; and W2 = the impact of the intervention on nutrition). Both weights were developed on the basis of expert interviews and technical consultation with experts from multiple ministries. Nutrition financing was determined by multiplying W1 by W2 in the budget line item.
8. Another emerging methodology that is currently being discussed within the SUN Donor Network is the use of the Organisation for Economic Co-operation and Development's Nutrition Policy Markers developed in 2018 on the basis of the donor resource tracking principles of (1) policy relevant, (2) technically accurate and evidence-based, (3) timely and reliable, (4) long-term, (5) standardized, and (6) transparent (USAID Advancing Nutrition, forthcoming). According to this methodology, donors review a project and give it a score of 0, 1, or 2 depending on the nutrition objective identified within the project: 0 = project does not target nutrition at all; 1 = project has significant nutrition objective (in which nutrition is a deliberate objective, but not the main reason for undertaking the project); and 2 = project has a principal nutrition objective. Once these scores are assigned, then the donors report on costs for projects with scores of 1 or 2 as nutrition expenditures.
9. Both options still involve a subjective assessment based on the practitioners' judgment, and the process could jeopardize replicability and transparency if it is complicated and the procedure is not documented adequately.
10. Fracassi et al. (2020) list the following typologies of normative weights that have been attempted by various countries: the dual approach (25 percent for sensitive and 100 percent specific); and the quadruple system (25 percent, 50 percent, 75 percent, and 100 percent).

11. In the 2020 updated supplemental guidance, SUN states that assigning weights is subjective, imprecise, and confusing, and that its only merit is that the exercise of assigning weights brings stakeholders together to look closely at their budgets and programs, which can sensitize them to each ministry's or agency's contribution to nutrition (MQSUN+ 2020).
12. None of the existing NPERs has properly assessed effectiveness by referencing any country-level impact evaluations or using other proxy means.
13. However, such comparison should always come with a caveat because there is no uniformity on what to include as nutrition spending, whether salaries and large capital investment such as infrastructure are included, on approaches to use of weights, and so on.
14. Agricultural expenditures are tracked and reported regularly at https://www.nepad.org/caadp/tracking-progress.
15. Another emerging category currently being discussed within the SUN Donor Network is direct/indirect nutrition activities (USAID Advancing Nutrition, forthcoming). USAID Advancing Nutrition (forthcoming) does not include the definition of direct/indirect nutrition activities but includes an indicative list. Direct nutrition activities are broken down into (1) direct health care sector nutritional interventions (for example, maternal and child micronutrient supplementation, including home fortification and delayed cord clamping); and (2) other sectoral strategies directly affecting nutrition (for example, iodized or micronutrient fortified salt and nutritional interventions in schools). Similarly, indirect nutrition activities are broken down into (1) indirect health care sector nutritional interventions (for example, family planning and reproductive health services, disease prevention, and management strategies, especially for diarrhea); and (2) other sectoral strategies indirectly affecting nutrition (for example, household food security and universal education, with a gender focus).
16. None of the existing NPERs has properly assessed effectiveness by referencing any country-level impact evaluations or using other proxy means.
17. Technical efficiency is sometimes also referred to as "cost efficiency" and measures efficiency in translating inputs into outputs for a given intervention.
18. Optima is open-source software developed by a network of academic partners, including the Burnet Institute, University College London, the University of Bern, and the University of New South Wales. Optima maintains disease-specific software for disease such as HIV, tuberculosis, and malaria, as well as nutrition (http://optimamodel.com/nutrition/).
19. Scenario 1: increasing the number of alive, nonstunted children; Scenario 2: increasing the number of alive, nonstunted, and nonanemic children; and Scenario 3: increasing the number of alive, nonstunted, and nonanemic children and minimizing anemia and mortality among pregnant women.
20. The forthcoming World Bank Health Public Expenditure Review Guidelines will include a cross-cutting note on technical efficiency analysis (Guidance on Assessing Spending Efficiency in the Health PER Guidelines).
21. None of the existing NPERs has properly assessed technical efficiency, mainly because of a lack of detailed within-program data. In fact, the Nepal and Tanzania NPERs specifically recommend the development of a data system with sufficient detailed categorization that would allow teams to carry out this analysis.
22. Some central-level allocations may be directed to regions to increase their share of spending. Because this information was not available, the data do not represent the full scope of subnational spending on malnutrition.
23. None of the NPERs examined for this guiding framework has carried out a BIA, mainly because of the lack of service delivery and expenditure data broken down by different income groups, as well as lack of precedence to follow in terms of an established methodology.
24. Living Standards Surveys are designed primarily to measure household income and expenditures rather than to collect health-related data. Information on the use of health services in these surveys is dependent on self-reported recent illnesses. This means that the information is collected only if respondents indicate that they or another household member had been ill or injured within a specified recall period, and the information is collected only in relation to that self-reported illness or injury episode. Therefore, health service use for other services beyond the recall period is not recorded, which leads to an incomplete picture of service use (McIntyre and Ataguba 2011).
25. For details on BIA methods and analysis, see O'Donnell et al. (2008).

REFERENCES

ACF International, Save the Children, and SUN Senegal. 2017. "Nutrition Budget Advocacy: Handbook for Civil Society." Action Contre la Faim, Paris. https://www.actioncontrelafaim.org/en/publication/nutrition-budget-advocacy-handbook-for-civil-society/.

Ahmed, S., M. Bhattarai, D. Drakpa, L. Dzed, M. Ghimire, P. Lhazon, A. Tandon, and V. Ulep. 2020. "'What Gets Measured Gets Managed': Assessing Public Financing for Improving Nutrition Outcomes and Human Capital in Bhutan." Health, Nutrition, and Population Discussion Paper, World Bank, Washington, DC.

Black, R., C. Victora, S. Walker, Z. Bhutta, P. Christian, M. De Onis, R. Uauy, et al. 2013. "Maternal and Child Undernutrition and Overweight in Low-Income and Middle-Income Countries." *The Lancet* 382 (9890): 427–51.

Bhutta, Z., J. Das, A. Rizvi, M. Gaffey, N. Walker, A. Lartey, R. E. Black, et al. 2013. "Evidence-Based Interventions for Improvement of Maternal and Child Nutrition: What Can Be Done and at What Cost?" *The Lancet* 382 (9890): 452–77.

Demery, L. 2000. "Benefit Incidence: A Practitioner's Guide." World Bank, Washington, DC. https://documents.worldbank.org/en/publication/documents-reports/documentdetail/574221468135940764/benefit-incidence-a-practitioners-guide.

Development Initiatives. 2017. *Global Nutrition Report 2017: Nourishing the SDGs*. Bristol: Development Initiatives. https://globalnutritionreport.org/reports/2017-global-nutrition-report/.

Finance Division, Government of the Republic of Bangladesh and UNICEF (United Nations Children's Fund), 2019. *Bangladesh Public Expenditure Review on Nutrition*. Dhaka: Government of Bangladesh and UNICEF.

Fracassi P., C. Picanyol, W. Knechtel, M. D'Alimonte, A. Gary, A. Pomeroy-Stevens, and R. Watts. 2020. "Budget Analysis for Nutrition: Guidance Note for Countries (Update 2020)." Scaling Up Nutrition, Geneva.

Galasso, E., and A. Wagstaff. 2017. "The Economic Costs of Stunting and How to Reduce Them." Policy Research Note 5, World Bank, Washington, DC.

Horton, S., and R. Steckel. 2013. "Malnutrition: Global Economic Losses Attributable to Malnutrition 1900–2000 and Projections to 2050." In *How Much Have Global Problems Cost the World*, edited by Bjørn Lomborg, 247–72. Cambridge: Cambridge University Press.

Independent Evaluation Group. 2010. *What Can We Learn from Nutrition Impact Evaluations? Lessons from a Review of Interventions to Reduce Child Malnutrition in Developing Countries*. Washington, DC: World Bank.

Indonesia Ministry of National Development Planning, National Development Planning Agency, and Indonesia Ministry of Finance. 2018. "Guidelines for Tagging, Tracking and Evaluating Development and Budget Performance to Prevent Stunting—for Line Ministries/Agencies." Unpublished.

Masiye, F. 2007. "Investigating Health System Performance: An Application of Data Envelopment Analysis to Zambian Hospitals." *BMC Health Services Research*, April 25. https://doi.org/10.1186/1472-6963-7-58.

McIntyre, D., and J. Ataguba. 2011. "How to Do (or Not to Do) ... A Benefit Incidence Analysis." *Health Policy Plan* 26 (2): 174–82. https://pubmed.ncbi.nlm.nih.gov/20688764/.

MQSUN+ (Maximising the Quality of Scaling Up Nutrition Plus). 2020. "Supplemental Guidance for the SUN Budget Analysis: An Update for Countries (Feb. 2020)." MQSUN+, Washington, DC. https://mqsunplus.path.org/resources/supplemental-guidance-for-the-sun-budget-analysis/.

National Planning Commission. 2017. *Multi-Sector Nutrition Plan: 2018–2022*. Kathmandu: National Planning Commission. https://extranet.who.int/ncdccs/Data/NPL_B11_MSNPii.pdf.

O'Donnell, O., E. van Doorslaer, A. Wagstaff, and M. Lindelow. 2008. *Analyzing Health Equity Using Household Survey Data: A Guide to Techniques and Their Implementation*. Washington, DC: World Bank.

Piatti-Fünfkirchen, M., L. Liang, J. K. Akuoku, and P. Mwitende. 2020. "Rwanda Nutrition Expenditure and Institutional Review." World Bank, Washington, DC.

Shekar, M., J. Kakietek, J. Eberwein, and D. Walters. 2017. *An Investment Framework for Nutrition: Reaching the Global Targets for Stunting, Anemia, Breastfeeding, and Wasting*. Directions in Development—Human Development. Washington, DC: World Bank.

Shiell, A., C. Donaldson, C. Mitton, and G. Currie. 2002. "Health Economic Evaluation." *Journal of Epidemiology and Community Health* 56: 85–88.

Tanzania, MoFP (Ministry of Finance and Planning) and UNICEF (United Nations Children's Fund). 2018. "Nutrition Public Expenditure Review 2014–2016: Mainland Tanzania." MoFP and UNICEF, Dar es Salaam.

USAID Advancing Nutrition. Forthcoming. *Strengthening Donor Resource Tracking for Nutrition Across Sectors: Recommendations to the SDN on the Application and Interpretation of the OECD Nutrition Policy Marker*. Arlington, VA: USAID Advancing Nutrition.

World Bank. 2016a. "Ethiopia Public Expenditure Review." World Bank, Washington, DC. https://openknowledge.worldbank.org/handle/10986/24370.

World Bank. 2016b. "Mozambique Health Public Expenditure Review: 2009–2013." World Bank, Washington, DC.

World Bank. 2019a. "Assessing Public Financing for Nutrition in Nepal 2011–17." Unpublished report.

World Bank. 2019b. "Zambia Health Sector Public Expenditure Review: 2006–2016." World Bank, Washington, DC.

World Bank. 2020a. "Spending Better to Reduce Stunting in Indonesia: Findings from a Public Expenditure Review." World Bank, Washington, DC.

World Bank. 2020b. "Sri Lanka PER for Nutrition in Sri Lanka: Assessing Public Financing for Nutrition in Sri Lanka (2014–2018)." World Bank, Washington DC.

World Bank. Forthcoming. "Strengthening Accountability for Nutrition Results through Improved Public Financial Management." World Bank, Washington, DC.

Using the NPER for Greater Impact

Recommendations should directly follow the analysis (and not suddenly introduce a set of unrelated or unsubstantiated recommendations at the end of the nutrition public expenditure review [NPER] report). An NPER, regardless of its scope, should offer useful inputs into current and future decisions related to planning and budgetary management, with the objective to improve the quality and impact of public spending on nutrition. Recommendations derived from the results of an NPER analysis should (1) reflect country conditions and be consistent with national nutrition goals and objectives, (2) build upon ongoing initiatives, (3) identify cost implications or any clear trade-offs based on an evidence-based analysis, (4) separate short- and long-term recommendations, (5) separate recommendations by institution or audience, and (6) ensure appropriate time-sequencing. Recommendations should be presented in a format that most likely encourages uptake and implementation of the recommendations.

THE WAY FORWARD ON POLICY DIALOGUE AND INSTITUTIONAL STRENGTHENING

The fundamental benefit of an NPER is to provide an opportunity to extend the policy dialogue on nutrition to improve the implementation performance and impact of nutrition expenditures. The completion of a sound NPER is only the beginning of this process. If the NPER process ends at the final meeting or consultation workshop, the result is an informative report (obtained at a relatively high cost) of underused operational value. Thus, the NPER team must consider how the NPER will be disseminated and support the transition into tangible policy actions based on NPER recommendations.

Although NPERs build on the work of PERs, they are new tools that have only a limited portfolio of work to date. Therefore, this guiding framework should be considered a starting point to outlining an approach to carry out NPERs. It will undoubtedly undergo revision as NPER standard methodology is concretized and more NPER examples become available.

To improve the public financial management of nutrition expenditures at the country level once the NPER is completed (or concurrently), countries should consider the following:

- *Developing an action plan and budget to implement reforms identified in the NPER.* For example, evidence generated in NPERs could help policy makers identify underfunded programs or geographical, inefficient spending patterns (for example, large legacy programs such as food subsidies), and plans to reallocate spending to course correct.
- *Creating country-specific guidelines for tracking nutrition expenditures.* Definitions of nutrition spending at the country level may evolve over time as countries develop or data availability changes. It is important to document exactly what is included in the analysis to ensure that comparisons (over time) can be made. Countries need to recognize that tracking and evaluating nutrition-related expenditures will be an ongoing exercise, and new expenditure items will need to be tagged as they are included in the budget.
- *Strengthening or developing a tracking methodology for development partner (DP) financing that generates sufficiently disaggregated data for NPERs.* Collecting data on DP financing can be done through manual surveys, as is done in several countries. However, it would be useful if countries could improve DP financing tracking and monitoring mechanisms by, for example, creating an integrated DP financing module in the financial management information system or integrated financial management system (FMIS/IFMIS). Integrating the collection of off-budget data into the country's FMIS/IFMIS would make it easier to monitor DP financing flows and make corrective allocations.
- *Improving the visibility of nutrition-related expenditures in FMIS/IFMIS.* Potential measures to improve FMIS/IFMIS include (1) ensuring the proper budgetary tagging of nutrition-related expenditures, which can be done using relevant budgetary tracer line items that are routinely tracked; (2) unbundling nutrition interventions; (3) breaking down salaries and operating costs; and (4) providing insights into subnational allocations of central expenditures. This would help to institutionalize the estimation of public financing for nutrition as part of the routine to track public spending and implement programs. In addition, adequately mainstreaming nutrition tagging into the budget cycle will eliminate the need for assigning subjective disaggregation weights.
- *Strengthening the monitoring and evaluation function of nutrition-related programs and nutrition information collection within service delivery platforms.* The objective would be to ensure that nutrition programs consistently generate high-quality administrative data (to capture outputs and some outcomes) and that they periodically undergo impact evaluations to assess outcomes and impacts. Such evaluations would enable future NPERs to analyze the effectiveness and technical efficiency of nutrition interventions.

IMPROVING THE QUALITY OF FUTURE NPERs

To improve the quality of NPERs, policy makers and stakeholders of the global nutrition community should consider the following:

- *Developing a consensus on a common approach to deal with the issue of high-cost, nutrition-sensitive interventions.* Scaling Up Nutrition's guidance on whether to use weights on nutrition spending deals exclusively with the "bundled budget" problem—when nutrition-related activities are bundled with other non-nutrition-related activities. However, the existing portfolio of NPERs shows that many have used weights for a different purpose (that is, to discount for perceived low contribution to nutrition of some high-cost, nutrition-sensitive interventions). A global consensus is urgently needed to address the real problem that NPER teams face in assessing high-cost, nutrition-sensitive interventions (for example, infrastructure costs like water pipes, school toilets, and irrigation). To move this agenda forward, more work is needed to improve the inclusion criteria (Step 5 in the chapter 3 section on identifying nutrition expenditures) and conduct more research on the impact of high-cost, nutrition-sensitive interventions for possible use in future NPERs (for example, the alternative methodology piloted in Burkina Faso, as presented in Step 5 of the same section).
- *Generating more cross-country data to allow for international and regional comparisons, to benchmark progress, and to identify gaps in nutrition financing.* Generating such data will require more work to assess available data and refine or standardize methodologies,[1] including developing (1) a common classification system for nutrition-specific and nutrition-sensitive activities that can be accepted and consistently used by a diverse set of countries, and (2) inclusion criteria to screen high-cost, nutrition-sensitive interventions (related to the challenges around weighting). Because standardization needs to be based on evidence of what does and does not work, which is currently limited, there is a great need for generating more data from robust NPERs and assessing them for methodological consolidation.
- *Using data in an innovative way as the NPER portfolio grows to achieve a more detailed analysis and develop standard methodologies.* The current existing NPERs do not include types of analysis that are commonly seen in sector-specific public expenditure reviews, such as effectiveness analysis and technical efficiency analysis. As work continues on increasing the visibility of nutrition-related expenditures and evaluating the performance of nutrition programs, guidance on best practices for NPERs should also be continuously revisited to build up the knowledge base.

NOTE

1. A standardized methodology must always be evaluated to ensure it fits in the context of the country's specific nutrition priorities. This means that country-specific adjustments to standard tools (e.g., classification systems for nutrition-specific and -sensitive activities) or inclusion criteria may be needed. While this may limit the scope of the international comparability of the identified nutrition expenditures, basing the NPER on the country's own nutrition priorities and strategies is a fundamentally important principle to ensure that the outcome is relevant, and any resulting recommendations are actionable.

Framework for Actions to Achieve Optimum Fetal and Child Nutrition and Development, as Published in *The Lancet*

THE LANCET FRAMEWORK

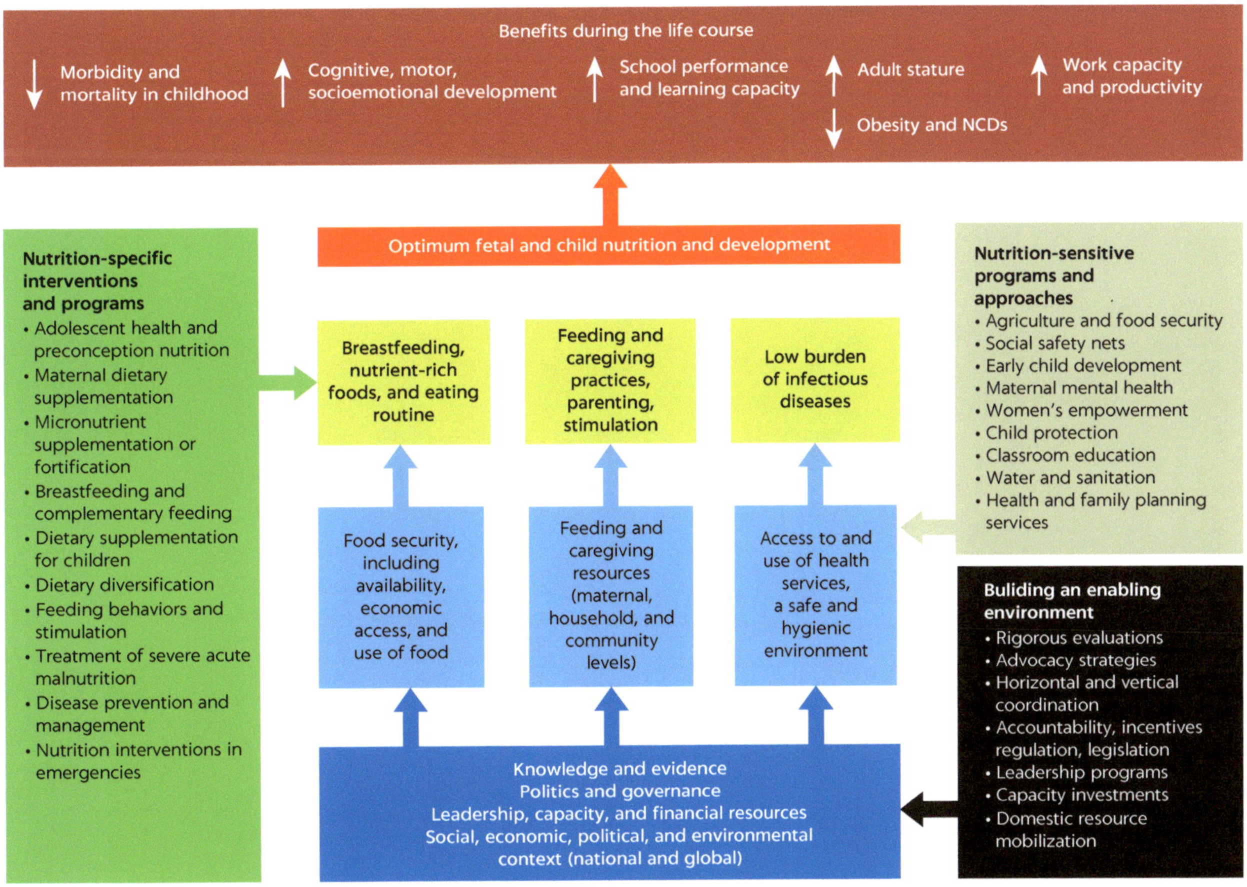

Benefits during the life course
- ↓ Morbidity and mortality in childhood
- ↑ Cognitive, motor, socioemotional development
- ↑ School performance and learning capacity
- ↑ Adult stature
- ↓ Obesity and NCDs
- ↑ Work capacity and productivity

Optimum fetal and child nutrition and development

Nutrition-specific interventions and programs
- Adolescent health and preconception nutrition
- Maternal dietary supplementation
- Micronutrient supplementation or fortification
- Breastfeeding and complementary feeding
- Dietary supplementation for children
- Dietary diversification
- Feeding behaviors and stimulation
- Treatment of severe acute malnutrition
- Disease prevention and management
- Nutrition interventions in emergencies

- Breastfeeding, nutrient-rich foods, and eating routine
- Feeding and caregiving practices, parenting, stimulation
- Low burden of infectious diseases

- Food security, including availability, economic access, and use of food
- Feeding and caregiving resources (maternal, household, and community levels)
- Access to and use of health services, a safe and hygienic environment

Nutrition-sensitive programs and approaches
- Agriculture and food security
- Social safety nets
- Early child development
- Maternal mental health
- Women's empowerment
- Child protection
- Classroom education
- Water and sanitation
- Health and family planning services

Knowledge and evidence
Politics and governance
Leadership, capacity, and financial resources
Social, economic, political, and environmental context (national and global)

Building an enabling environment
- Rigorous evaluations
- Advocacy strategies
- Horizontal and vertical coordination
- Accountability, incentives regulation, legislation
- Leadership programs
- Capacity investments
- Domestic resource mobilization

Source: Black et al. 2013. © Elsevier. Reproduced with permission from Elsevier; further permission required for reuse.
Note: NCDs = noncommunicable diseases.

REFERENCE

Black, R., C. Victora, S. Walker, Z. Bhutta, P. Christian, M. De Onis, R. Uauy, et al. 2013. "Maternal and Child Undernutrition and Overweight in Low-Income and Middle-Income Countries." *The Lancet* 382 (9890): 427–51.

Results Structure of the Nepal Multi-Sector Nutrition Plan: 2018–2022

GOAL (Impact): Improved maternal, adolescent, and child nutrition by scaling up essential nutrition-specific and nutrition-sensitive interventions and creating an enabling environment for nutrition

- Stunting prevalence
- Wasting prevalence
- Low birth weight prevalence
- % reduction in child overweight and obesity
- % reduction in overweight and obesity in reproductive-age women
- % women with chronic energy deficiency

Outcome 1: Improved access to and equitable use of nutrition-specific services

Indicators with targets:
- Increased % of children 6–23 months having minimum acceptable diet
- Increased % of children under 6 months with exclusive breastfeeding
- Reduced % of anemia among children 6–59 months
- Reduced % of anemia among adolescent girls (10–19 years)
- Reduced % of anemia among WRA (15–49 years)
- Reduced prevalence of under 5-year-old children with diarrhea in last two weeks
- Mean dietary diversity score among WRA (15–49 years)

Outcome 2: Improved access to and equitable use of nutrition-sensitive services and improved healthy habits and practices

Indicators with targets:
- Reduced proportion of population below minimum level of dietary energy consumption
- Increased % people using safe drinking water
- Increased % people using improved sanitation facilities that are not shared
- Increased % of people practicing hand washing with soap and water before feeding baby (0–2 years) and after cleaning babies' bottoms
- Percentage of women aged 20–24 years who were married or in union before age 18
- Increased gross enrollment rate (boys and girls) in early childhood education and development or in preprimary education
- Decreased % of out-of-school children (boys/girls) in basic education
- Increased basic education cycle completion rate (boys/girls)

Outcome 3: Improved policies, plans, and multisectoral coordination at federal, provincial, and local government levels to enhance the nutrition status of all population groups

Indicators with targets:
- % of farm land owned by women or in joint ownership
- No. of local, provincial and federal government plans that include nutrition and food security programs in line with MSNP-II
- Availability of national MSNP-II document
- Availability of national budget code for nutrition and food security
- National Capacity Development Master Plan for implementation of MSNP-II produced
- Multisector commitment and resources for nutrition increase to at least 3.5% of total government budget
- Financial resource tracking in place

[Example of a nutrition-specific output]
Output 1.X: Improved nutrition and care practices

Indicators with targets:
- % newborns initiating breastfeeding within 1 hour of birth
- Proportion of infants 6–8 months receiving solid, semi-solid, and soft foods
- % children 0–59 months who received more frequent feeding during episodes of diarrhea

Key activities with targets:
- Conduct maternal, infant, and young child nutrition counseling on all health sector platforms, such as health mother's group meetings, immunization, ANC, PNC, growth monitoring, PHC-ORC, IMNCI and OPD
- Conduct regular growth monitoring counseling at PHC-ORCs and health facilities
- Regularly disseminate IEC/BCC materials in line with Food Based Dietary Guidelines through health facilities, FCHVs to communities and households
- Engage media for documentation and dissemination of MIYCN program
• • • • •

[Example of a nutrition-sensitive output]
Output 2.X: Increased physical and economic access to diversified food

Indicators with targets:
- Improved access to updated agriculture marketing information
- Publish agriculture marketing information bulletin (once a year)
- Updated website and app related to agriculture marketing information system
- Households raising livestock

Key activities with targets:
- Enhance access and use of animal source foods
  - Open market establishments (#)
  - Chilling vat distribution (#)
  - Awareness programs to use safe animal products (events)
- Promote and support production and consumption of fish including support to establish community ponds for production and local consumption (tons)

[Example of an enabling environment output]
Output 3.X: Functional updated information system across the sectors

Indicators with targets:
- MSNP-II M&E framework developed or updated for all sectors and implemented at federal, provincial, and local levels
- Web-based reporting system linked with MSNP-II M&E plan at all levels (7 sectors)
- NNFSS portal updated each quarter
- No. of sectoral reports updated on NNFSS portal as per M&E plan each quarter

Key activities with targets:
- Update MSNP information portal and make it functional
- Link and update nutrition information at central level (HMIS, EMIS, WASH agriculture, livestock and local governance)
- Provide training on web-based MSNP reporting system at federal and provincial level
- Develop/review M&E framework for all MSNP sectors at fedral level
- Develop/review M&E framework for all MSNP sectors at provincial level
- Develop M&E framework for all MSNP sectors at local level
• • • • •

Source: National Planning Commission 2017.

Note: ANC = antenatal care; EMIS = Education Management Information System; FCHV = female community health volunteer; HMIS = Health Management Information System; IEC/BCC = information education and communication/behavior change communication; IMNCI = management of childhood illness; M&E = monitoring and evaluation; MSNP-II = Multi-Sector Nutrition Plan: 2018–2022; MIYCN = maternal, infant, and young child undernutrition; NNFSS = National Nutrition and Food Security Secretariat; OPD = outpatient department; PHC-ORC = primary health care outreach clinic; PNC = postnatal care; WASH = water, sanitation, and hygiene; WRA = women of reproductive age.

REFERENCE

National Planning Commission. 2017. *Multi-Sector Nutrition Plan: 2018–2022*. Kathmandu: National Planning Commission. https://extranet.who.int/ncdccs/Data/NPL_B11_MSNP ii.pdf.

List of NPERs and Other Related Documents

This appendix contains lists of nutrition public expenditure reviews (NPERs) and known related documents. There could be other documents, especially by non–World Bank entities, that are not listed here.

TABLE C.1 Nutrition public expenditure reviews

COUNTRY	YEAR	ORGANIZATION	TITLE
Bangladesh	2019	United Nations Children's Fund	Bangladesh Public Expenditure Review on Nutrition
Bhutan	2020	World Bank	"What Gets Measured Gets Managed": Assessing Public Financing for Improving Nutrition Outcomes and Human Capital in Bhutan
Indonesia	2020	World Bank	Spending Better to Reduce Stunting in Indonesia: Findings from a Public Expenditure Review
Nepal	2019	World Bank	Assessing Public Financing for Nutrition in Nepal 2011–17 (unpublished)
Rwanda	2020	World Bank	Rwanda Nutrition Expenditure and Institutional Review 2020
Sri Lanka	2020	World Bank/United Nations Children's Fund	Assessing Public Financing for Nutrition in Sri Lanka 2014–18
Tanzania	2018	United Nations Children's Fund	Nutrition Public Expenditure Review 2014–2016: Mainland Tanzania

Sources: Ahmed et al. 2020; Finance Division, Government of the Republic of Bangladesh and UNICEF 2018; Piatti-Fünfkirchen et al. 2020; Tanzania, MoFP and UNICEF 2018; World Bank 2019a, 2020a, 2020b.

TABLE C.2 Related documents: nutrition financing tracking, sector public expenditure reviews with nutrition coverage

COUNTRY	YEAR	ORGANIZATION	TITLE
Ethiopia	No date	Results for Development (R4D)	Tracking Funding for Nutrition in Ethiopia Across Sectors
Ethiopia	2021	World Bank	Assessment of woreda-level budget, planning process, and flow of funding in human capital sectors (unpublished internal working paper)
Lesotho	2019	World Bank	Agriculture Public Expenditure Review
Mozambique	2016	World Bank	Mozambique Health Public Expenditure Review: 2009–2013 (unpublished)
Pakistan*	2019	World Bank	Nutrition Expenditure Tracking in Pakistan Guidelines (unpublished)
Paraguay	No date	World Bank	Una revisión del gasto público en primera infancia en Paraguay (in Spanish, unpublished)
Rwanda	2016	World Bank	Volume II: Expenditure Analysis of Selected Strategic Topics Using the AgPER Lite Methodology (unpublished)
Zambia	2018	World Bank	Zambia Health Sector Public Expenditure Review

Sources: Chansa et al. 2018; FMoH, n.d.; Policy Associates Team 2016; World Bank 2016, 2019b, 2019c.
Note: * = guidance document only.

REFERENCES

Ahmed, S., M. Bhattarai, D. Drakpa, L. Dzed, M. Ghimire, P. Lhazon, A. Tandon, and V. Ulep. 2020. "'What Gets Measured Gets Managed': Assessing Public Financing for Improving Nutrition Outcomes and Human Capital in Bhutan." Health, Nutrition, and Population Discussion Paper, World Bank, Washington, DC.

Chansa, C., N. W. Workie, M. Piatti, T. Matsebula, and K. J. Yoo. 2018. "Zambia Health Sector Public Expenditure Review." World Bank, Washington, DC.

Finance Division, Government of the Republic of Bangladesh and UNICEF (United Nations Children's Fund), 2018. *Bangladesh Public Expenditure Review on Nutrition.* Dhaka: Government of Bangladesh and UNICEF.

FMoH (Federal Republic of Ethiopia Ministry of Health). No date. "Tracking Funding for Nutrition in Ethiopia across Sectors: Ethiopian Fiscal Years 2006 to 2008 (2013/14 to 2015/16)." FMoH, Addis Ababa.

Piatti-Fünfkirchen, M., L. Liang, J. K. Akuoku, and P. Mwitende. 2020. "Rwanda Nutrition Expenditure and Institutional Review." World Bank, Washington, DC.

Policy Associates Team. 2016. "Expenditure Analysis of Selected Strategic Topics Using the AgPER Lite Methodology, Volume II." Unpublished report.

Tanzania, MoFP (Ministry of Finance and Planning) and UNICEF (United Nations Children's Fund). 2018. "Nutrition Public Expenditure Review 2014–2016: Mainland Tanzania." MoFP and UNICEF, Dar es Salaam.

World Bank. No date. "Una revisión del gasto público en primera infancia en Paraguay." Unpublished report.

World Bank. 2016. "Mozambique Health Public Expenditure Review 2009–2013." Unpublished report.

World Bank. 2019a. "Assessing Public Financing for Nutrition in Nepal." Unpublished report.

World Bank. 2019b. "Kingdom of Lesotho: Agriculture Public Expenditure Review." World Bank, Washington, DC.

World Bank. 2019c. "Pakistan Nutrition Expenditure Tracking Guidelines." Unpublished report.

World Bank. 2020a. "Spending Better to Reduce Stunting in Indonesia: Findings from a Public Expenditure Review." World Bank, Washington, DC.

World Bank. 2020b. "Sri Lanka PER for Nutrition in Sri Lanka: Assessing Public Financing for Nutrition in Sri Lanka (2014–2018)." World Bank, Washington DC.